SETBACK LEADERSHIP

How leaders turn their setbacks into successes. And how you can, too!

SRIJATA BHATNAGAR

INDIA • SINGAPORE • MALAYSIA

Notion Press

Old No. 38, New No. 6
McNichols Road, Chetpet
Chennai - 600 031

First Published by Notion Press 2019
Copyright © Srijata Bhatnagar 2019
All Rights Reserved.

ISBN 978-1-64678-707-4

This book has been published with all efforts taken to make the material error-free after the consent of the author. However, the author and the publisher do not assume and hereby disclaim any liability to any party for any loss, damage, or disruption caused by errors or omissions, whether such errors or omissions result from negligence, accident, or any other cause.

While every effort has been made to avoid any mistake or omission, this publication is being sold on the condition and understanding that neither the author nor the publishers or printers would be liable in any manner to any person by reason of any mistake or omission in this publication or for any action taken or omitted to be taken or advice rendered or accepted on the basis of this work. For any defect in printing or binding the publishers will be liable only to replace the defective copy by another copy of this work then available.

Disclaimer: This book contains personal stories of leaders from various fields, geographies and age groups, along with the author's interpretation of the key lessons that these stories offer. Each story is narrated in the words of the person concerned.

The author has done her best to make sure that every story is authentic and original, and that every piece of information in this book is correct. Any similarity with anybody else's stories or words, if it exists, is purely coincidental. The names of some secondary characters in the stories have been changed to protect their privacy.

If you find a factual error in this book, please bring it to the notice of the publisher or author, for them to take corrective action.

Dedication

I dedicate this book to all those whom I have met, coached and trained in the last 20 years of my professional life – people who went through various setbacks and yet, instead of succumbing to them, turned them into their breakthroughs.

I dedicate it to my parents, who taught me to be strong and to take setbacks head-on.

I dedicate it to my husband for being my best cheerleader and allowing me to learn every lesson on my way, falling and failing. Thank you for letting me be myself.

I dedicate it to my daughters – one of them poses challenges, while the other teaches me how to make the most of those challenges.

I dedicate it to my father-in-law, who is my inspiration, friend, philosopher and guide; whose army-day stories taught me unique ways of dealing with setbacks. Love you, daddy!

I dedicate it to the entire defence force of India.

Email me your selfie with the book and your Facebook profile link to get added in the closed group of Setback Leaders for continuous learning. Because Setback Leadership is a LIFESTYLE for a truly successful life.

connect@srijatabhatnagar.com

Contents

Gratitude does matter! 7
Introduction – Who Wants a Setback, Anyway? 9

Chapter 1.   The Earlier, The Better 17

Chapter 2.   Workplace Woes 33

Chapter 3.   The Broken Heart Syndrome 45

Chapter 4.   Square Peg in a Round Hole 59

Chapter 5.   Venture Misadventure 71

Chapter 6.   Capital Mistakes 85

Chapter 7.   A Single Stab, A Hundred Wounds 95

Chapter 8.   Death and Beyond 105

Chapter 9.   Do or Die! 113

Final Words – Let's Recap and Practice the Techniques 129
About the Author 133

Gratitude does matter!

When I have so many people to be grateful to, how can I thank them all in such a limited space? Still, I am going to attempt it.

I am thankful to all my clients. This book was written because of them. If I hadn't been intrigued by their questions and life-challenges, this book wouldn't have happened at all.

Big hugs and thanks to all those who encouraged me to write this book – my husband, Aneesh Bhatnagar, my friends Pravin Shekar, Neha Tripathi, Krishne Gowda and others.

I am forever indebted to all the contributors who willingly shared their stories and experiences – Brandi Benson, Diaz Richards, Katherine Wintsch, Dr Kuiljeit Uppaal, Lauren Powers, Nikhil Chaudhary, Roger Cheetham and Sagar Amlani. I know it isn't easy to share your setbacks with the world. But you did it wholeheartedly. And thank you for that.

Deep gratitude to those who offered to read the initial manuscript of this book and give constructive feedback. You know who you are.

High-fives, hugs and thanks to my editor, Ganesh Vancheeswaran, and cover designer, Arun Ramkumar, without whom this book wouldn't have come out this way.

Gratitude to Notion Press for publishing this book in the best possible way, keeping all my specifications in mind.

THANK YOU!

Introduction – Who Wants a Setback, Anyway?

One morning in July 2019, India woke up to the shocking news that VG Siddhartha, the founder of India's largest coffee chain, Café Coffee Day, had gone missing. This was quickly followed by news of his death, with reports speculating that he had taken his own life. In the note he left behind, Siddhartha had written, "I have failed as an entrepreneur". Café Coffee Day is the Indian equivalent of Starbucks and Siddhartha was a visionary entrepreneur who had created 50,000 jobs in 37 years of running a business successfully. If a leader like him felt the way he did, there is something terribly wrong in the way we look at success, failure and setbacks, and in how we deal with them! What's especially unfortunate is that in many cases, even the closest support system doesn't help the affected person. In Siddhartha's case, his family was completely unaware of his anguished state of mind! When even such great business leaders choose this way to deal with setbacks, it's time to go back to the basics and take a fresh look at our attitude to setbacks and challenges – this time, from a completely different perspective.

> And that's what this book is all about – seeing severe setbacks in a different perspective and learning how to overcome them and find success. As you will see in the subsequent pages, a setback offers us a wonderful opportunity for transforming our life. Equipped with the right techniques and mindset, we can come back strongly from a setback and lead a fulfilling life.

I see so many people get hit by setbacks. Most of them give up in some way or the other. Even worse, some of them kill themselves, unable to cope with the setbacks and society's response to them. These incidents have always broken my heart.

I have seen men who have lost their jobs being ridiculed by their own families. I have also seen girls who chose to break out of abusive or unfulfilling relationships being asked embarrassing questions and being judged by their families. I have seen husbands judging their wives' ability to manage money better and ironically, contributing to the loss of money themselves. I have seen parents being extraordinarily harsh with kids who failed in an exam. Leave alone failing; sometimes, not making it to the top grade is enough to unleash the wrath of the parents on the poor children. I have seen entrepreneurs succumb to the harsh realities of the start-up world.

> **PAUSE AND REFLECT**
>
> What has been your experience with your closest support system when you hit a rough patch? Did you receive any help from them? How did that help you deal with your setback?
>
> Jot down your responses in your notepad and reflect over them for a minute.
>
> Also, share them with me by writing to me at connect @srijatabhatnagar.com

Setbacks – An Inevitable Part of Life

I am yet to come across a single person who has never faced a setback, however small or big it may have been. Every human being goes through challenges – personal, professional, emotional or otherwise. Someone loses a loved one, someone fails in a significant professional exam, someone loses a job, someone gets rejected in love, someone has a bad time with their finances, someone goes through bad relationships and so on. You know what? I have been through most of these setbacks myself. Falling, failing, getting ridiculed and finally learning to get up, walk and soar. My journey has been a long and tough one, but definitely a fulfilling one.

> Interestingly, we tend to think that successful people never go through setbacks. We idolise successful people, assuming they have had a setback-free life. This is nothing but a myth. Let's take a few world-famous personalities and peep into their early lives, shall we?

Whether it is JK Rowling – one of UK's most influential women and a blockbuster author; India's magnificent Mary Kom – the only woman to win the World Amateur Boxing Championship eight times; Steve Jobs – the technology maven and co-founder of Apple; or Sachin Tendulkar – the legendary Indian batsman who is hailed as the God of Cricket, they have all had their share of serious setbacks.

Rowling's is a classic example of the 'rags to riches' story. She was once living on England's welfare benefits (dole) and thought of herself as a failure. Her marriage had failed and she was jobless, with a dependent child to boot. At one point of time, she was diagnosed with clinical depression and even contemplated suicide. Her first book in the Harry Potter series was rejected by every single publisher she approached, until, finally, it was picked up by Scholastic, a publishing house. From living on dole to becoming a billionaire author, Rowling has undoubtedly had a phenomenal journey. (Source: Wikipedia)

Steve Jobs was thrown out of Apple, but made a convincing comeback a few years later, when he picked up the reins of the company as the CEO. He succeeded in rescuing the company from the verge of bankruptcy. (Source: Wikipedia) How many entrepreneurs show the courage to join the same company that threw them out earlier and eventually become the reason for its huge success?

Mary Kom comes from a humble background. She lives in Manipur, a small state in the north-eastern corner of India. Though she married early and had children, she chose to return to her professional dreams quickly. Whereas people in most parts of the world think that women should solely concentrate on family and childbearing after marriage, Mary Kom broke all stereotypes to become the World Amateur Boxing champion a record number of times. (Source: Wikipedia)

Sachin Tendulkar was blessed with unique talent right from childhood and got the right exposure early on. Thanks to his rapid rise as a batsman par excellence, he came to be known as the 'God of Cricket'. And yet, the world's best batsman couldn't achieve much in his role as captain of the Indian cricket team. Ultimately, he had to resign this post to focus on his batting. (Source: Wikipedia)

The point is, it is not necessary that just because someone is very successful in one role, they will be successful every time in every situation or in different roles. People can never be fail-proof.

I invite you to do a Google search on any celebrity and read their life story carefully. You will be surprised to find the kind of setbacks each one of them has faced or is still facing. The fact is, the more successful a person becomes, the larger their setbacks are. Why only famous personalities, let's delve into the lives of people like us and see what they have gone through in their lives. Let's see if we can get inspired by them.

> **PAUSE AND REFLECT**
>
> Here is a task for you. Pick three successful people from your circle and either ask them if they have faced any setbacks in life or do a quick research on them. I know for sure that you will find some interesting and surprising answers.

There is just no way to avoid setbacks from coming into our lives. And yet, I see a lot of people dreading setbacks and failures the way they dread death!

Our Flawed Thinking

If setbacks are inevitable, why do people dread them? Also, why do they distance themselves from those who are going through setbacks? Have you ever thought about it?

Well, it comes from the flawed thinking that a person going through a setback is not 'good enough' or is a failure. They are thought to be less capable than others and seen as under-achievers. Or, we say that they didn't put in their best effort and that's why they are facing challenges. There is a stigma attached to setbacks, whether they are to do with education, career, love, relationships, losing money, losing a loved one or any other aspect of life. Every time someone goes through a rough patch in their life, they get ridiculed and are looked down upon. Others are told not to be like them.

What happens when such societal pressure engulfs a person who is going through a rough patch in life? No prizes for guessing. They sink even low in confidence, withdraw themselves from the world and avoid facing people and situations. Why, they even deny that the tough situation exists! Sometimes, they manage to put up a fake brave face, in the hope of approval from family, friends and colleagues. Our society and our education system teach us how to be strong. They also teach us *how* to succeed. **But, they don't teach us how to gracefully accept setbacks and failure, and stand up again to make a fresh start!** They don't recognise the precious learnings that come along with failures, setbacks and challenges. Have you ever seen parents teach their children how to face failure in life? Have you seen schools prepare their students to deal with failure? What about corporate organisations – do they deal with underachieving employees sensitively?

That's why we see so many people go into depression or even worse, kill themselves when they fail in an exam, go through a break-up, lose a job, are unable to repay debts or lose money in business. More than the incident itself, people are worried about the world's reactions to that incident. More than worrying about their wellbeing, they are thinking *"What will people say?"*, *"What will people think?"* and *"What if people laugh at me?"*

A Fresh Perspective to Empower You

So why read about setbacks at all, when everyone wants to avoid them? That's because SETBACKS ARE GOOD! You read that right. Repeat with me – SETBACKS ARE AWESOME!

Here is an open secret. No matter how much you want to avoid them, setbacks, failures, and challenges are part and parcel of life. They will come at some point or the other in your life to shake you up. Therefore, the smart thing to do is to be ready to overcome them as quickly and smoothly as possible. And this book will tell you how. Because, on the other side of setbacks lie great rewards. That's why you should see them from a different perspective, learn the techniques to handle them constructively and eventually, see the opportunity hidden in every setback.

Failure is an essential part of our growth and success – contrary to the popular belief that if you want to be successful, you should not have failed in earlier attempts. Think of setbacks, challenges and failure as speed breakers that life throws in your way. All you can do is to prepare yourself to handle them as efficiently as possible, without being bogged down by the 'noise' of the outer world or by your inner fears. Many organisations have started looking at this ability as an essential parameter while hiring, to assess how a person deals with failure.

> **I am not exaggerating one bit when I say that every setback is a potential leadership breakthrough. Are you tapping into its potential?**

Thanks to the nature of my work, I meet some incredibly successful people. Do you know the one thing that is common to all of them? *They have all had an unbelievable number of setbacks in their lives, but they decided to see past those setbacks.* They found opportunities in every setback and pursued them for their leadership breakthroughs.

How Will Setback Leadership Help You?

This book is a humble attempt to help you do the same; to learn from other great minds about how they dealt with their challenges in life and became today's invincible leaders. I have purposely chosen to interview those people whose life stories are just like yours and mine, but who are successful leaders in their respective fields today. So, you can completely relate to them. The people I have written about in this book are regular people from all over the world. What's extraordinary about them is that they converted their setbacks into successes. You can be like them too, if you choose to.

Through this book, you will be able to dive deep into the minds of these leaders and learn the tools and strategies they used to handle setbacks like a pro. So, when *you* are attacked by setbacks, you can manage them like a pro, too. In the chapters to come, we will talk about the different kinds of major setbacks people usually encounter, read stories of people who have successfully overcome similar setbacks and learn from them. I hope this will help you reach for the sky. Remember, leadership is a mindset and attitude; it is not a position or pay grade.

Just Imagine. When you have learnt the skills and tricks to handle setbacks in the most productive and least damaging way, how will your life be? What if you didn't have to go through the destructive thoughts that you generally go through when faced with a challenge? What if you knew how to proudly face the world (instead of hiding from it) in the face of a debacle? What if you could learn some powerful life lessons and be able to use them to become a leader?

With the help of this book, I see you overcoming any significant setback you face at any point of time and coming out victorious. Much like a swimmer who finds himself under a huge wave. When he is equipped with the right attitude, skills and strategies, he can crest the wave in a few seconds and swim away effortlessly.

Be the swimmer who tackles huge waves with confidence and crests them each time!

CHAPTER 1

The Earlier, The Better

> "What has been your earliest memory of a setback? How did you respond to it?"

When I asked a few successful leaders this question, they came back with unbelievably surprising answers. Some of them had not only faced setbacks early in life, but had to also figure out, through trial and error, how to overcome them.

DR KUILJEIT UPPAAL

Dr Kuiljeit Uppaal (http://www.kuiljeituppaal.com/) is the World's First Image Scientist. Among other things, she is a CEO, entrepreneur, aviator, Creative Director, author and educationist. Her multi-faceted career mastery has earned her the prestigious Inspirational Polymath Award. She has been featured in many records, including World Records India, Asia Book of Records and others, for being the world's first Image Scientist. She has been honoured with the 'Inspirational Educator Award' at the World Education Summit 2018 and the 'National Award for Innovative Concept' for her creation, PIQ. Kuiljeit received the prestigious honour of 'Pride of Maharashtra' in 2017.

She calls herself a curious person and credits her achievements to her curious self. Over the course of 25 years, she has dabbled in many things. Her journey started with aviation, moved to advertising – making movies and tapping into her creative side – and then to media and publication houses. She then worked in IT and later moved to Education, involving herself in the creation of a few hundred educational books in diverse areas. And finally, she moved into the world of research, where she continues to explore and develop path-breaking tools and methodologies for the benefit of the masses.

But all this didn't start easy for her. Early in her life, she suffered from polio. She narrates her story this way:

> *"When I was about six months old, I suffered a bout of polio. Neither my family nor the doctors came to know of it until I started walking and was in Kindergarten. Seeing me walk differently, my parents realised something was wrong. I would walk differently because one of my legs was much weaker than the other. When I started going to primary school, that was the first time I too realised there was some problem with my leg and that I wasn't like other normal kids. At school and outside, people started calling me all kinds of names, like the lame horse and so on. I was physically challenged in comparison with others, and I faced emotional lows when people made fun of me, teased me and called me different weird names.*

I was very fond of sports, and loved running and playing around. But, at sports in school, though I wanted to win a race, I couldn't. Leave alone winning; I would be one of the last ones even to complete the race! My weak leg didn't allow me to fulfil my desires. My aspirations were high; I wanted to run and do gymnastics and dance and play any sport. I tried to do all the things that other kids did, and as well as they did, but fell short. I realised that to fulfil my aspirations, I had to strengthen my leg a lot. Without doing that, I wouldn't be able to achieve my dreams.

I was about 9 or 10 years old when my dad put me into an athletics course to probably strengthen my leg. That's when my journey of overcoming my physical challenge started. Fortunately, I had an ambitious mind, and my desire to do well in sports and dance and every possible physical activity made me decide to overcome my physical challenge. When I realised I had a physical disability, I did go through an emotional challenge, as well. I did ask myself, 'Why me?' When everyone else had been given a perfectly healthy and normal body, why is it that I had to go through such a challenge at such a young age? I think it's reasonable to have such thoughts. But I never remained in that space for too long. I guess I was too young to nurture negative thinking in my mind. I quickly came out of the self-pity zone. I must have nudged my father at times, saying, 'I want to do this, but I can't. Why can't I?' Fortunately, I never felt self-pity.

After years of resilience and working hard on my leg, people would now be surprised to know that I ever had polio. I would smile and think in my head, 'How would you know? I have worked damn hard on my legs.' I ended up taking part in all the races I wanted to and emerged as a classical dancer, long jump champion, national-level athlete, parade commander, NCC best cadet, pilot and probably everything else I wanted to be! I think my legs have proven their worth in all the possible places they needed to, as I now moved from being ordinary to extraordinary.

Challenges and setbacks are like friends; they come and teach us something new, and give us opportunities to enhance ourselves quickly. I thank God for the challenges he gave me. Every time I overcome a challenge, I pat myself on the back and say to Almighty, 'I am truly your loved child,' because I feel God has given me the power and wisdom to identify the challenge as a process of self-evolution.

To people who think they can't get past a setback in their life, it is my suggestion to walk out of the 'emotional' zone. Collect yourself, dwell in the zone for a maximum of only a few minutes; if you want to be overly kind to yourself, stay in that zone for five minutes and then get out of it. After that, be like a fly on the wall. Because when you do that, you are viewing the entire scenario pragmatically. And when you do this, you will discover your inner wisdom and the smartness of your brain to find solutions to your challenge quickly. It may not give you an ideal choice, but it will surely give you apt directions in which you can move forward. Always remember that the reason God placed your head above your heart is that they need to be used in that same order."

I can't even imagine the plight of a small child who realised she couldn't fulfil her dreams, simply because one of her legs was weak. Can you? From being oblivious about this setback to recognising and acknowledging it, and then deciding to work on it because she wanted to achieve her dreams – it has been quite a journey for Kuiljeit! Fortunately, she was a child when this happened and was uninhibited by society. Sometimes, I marvel at what a brilliant tool our mind is and what all we can achieve, if only we pointed it in the right direction. Are you using this fantastic tool right?

KATHERINE WINTSCH

Katherine Wintsch is the founder of The Mom Complex (https://momcomplex.com/) and the best-selling author of '*Slay Like A Mother*'. She is a professional speaker and a fearless leader. After more than ten years of studying mothers around the world and becoming one herself, she launched 'The Mom Complex' to develop better products and services that would make the lives of mothers more comfortable. Katherine's work is trusted by companies like Walmart, Unilever, Johnson & Johnson, The Discovery Network and Playskool. Her research has been featured on The Today Show, The New York Times, The Wall Street Journal and others. She regularly writes on modern motherhood through her blog 'In All Honesty' and her articles in The Huffington Post and Working Mother Magazine.

Today, Katherine takes care of all the chaos around her with calm and ease. But when she was an adolescent, she found it challenging to manoeuvre around the turmoil in her mind. She recalls her first setback clearly.

> *"My first experience with conditional love was my first significant setback in my life. I was just 15 years old when my first love, Daniel, told me one day that he didn't love me anymore. At that moment, what my young mind heard was that I wasn't loveable. In adolescence, kids anyway struggle to understand their identity and here, I was hearing from someone that he didn't love me. As a result, my dragon of self-doubt was born and it grew inside my head. I had to battle it for years to come, in every sphere of life.*
>
> *Faced by this challenge, my perfectionist tendency kicked into overdrive. I responded to every situation by going above and beyond, trying hard to be perfect, trying to fit in and do my best of best – even if that meant harming myself. This was my approach everywhere – in school, my personal life and my professional life. It was as if I was trying to prove to the world and myself that I'm worth loving. The harder I tried, the more unhappy I felt within. I was seeking external approval, and I thought that achievements, awards and accolades were the only ways to earn that approval.*
>
> *At that time, I didn't realise that true happiness doesn't lie in others' approval. Life is not only about awards and accolades; it is also about how much you love yourself. I had stopped loving myself, simply because someone else had stopped loving me. And because I had stopped loving myself, I felt the world had stopped loving me.*
>
> *It took me a long time, lots of deep learning, unlearning old beliefs and meditation to finally come to terms with the truth that success and contentment come from within me."*

I see a lot of my clients face the same issue of self-doubt and try extra hard to please everyone or to prove themselves to others. One of my clients once asked me, *"Srijata, every girl I like runs away from me. Am*

I not worthy of love?" Self-doubt and self-loathing are like acid. They corrode your very spirit over a period of time.

> **People do think that achievements, awards and accolades are the only ways to earn external approval that will eventually lead them to success. On the contrary, the constant need for approval and accolades actually traps them in a never-ending loop of struggle, ultimately putting them at the mercy of others.**

What they miss is the fact that successful people don't achieve something because of somebody else. They do it because **they themselves** want to do it. Success isn't a yardstick that the world should decide for you. You should define your success and achieve it for yourself.

SAGAR AMLANI

Sagar Amlani (https://www.linkedin.com/in/sagar-amlani/) is the host of LinkedInLocalHyderabad. He rose from the slums of Mumbai, defying all odds. Today, he is the Vice President of Fenoplast Limited in India. He is an expert on the topic 'Power of networking' and is a featured alumnus of Middlesex University, London. He was selected for the British Council leadership program, Dubai. He is one of the Limitless heroes of TEDx Hyderabad. His diverse qualifications include ePGDM (IIM, Kozhikode), MBA (Middlesex University), Chartered Chemical Engineer, Lead Auditor (ISO 9001), Internal Auditor (IATF), Certified Trainer (5s, Kaizen, Six Sigma – GB) and TRIZ (IIT Mumbai). Sagar regularly speaks at many small and medium enterprises, colleges and corporates. He is writing a book based on his overwhelming life story.

Sagar shares with us one of his earliest and deadliest setbacks that shaped him as a person and provided the fuel for his immense growth.

> *"For twelve years of my life, from middle school to my early days as a professional, we lived in a tiny chawl (a kind of tenement accommodating several residents) in the suburbs of Mumbai. Mumbai is famous for its chawls, where the rooms are generally around 10 ft high, the roof is made of asbestos sheet and a common corridor connects many houses. These are reasonable housing options for lower-middle-class families. Though each home is virtually like a matchbox, it was a concrete house where we could live at a very reasonable price.*
>
> *However, during the monsoons, it becomes challenging to live there. It is normal to have 3 to 6 inches of water flooding our chawl every monsoon, which would last about three months. We would use a dust scooper to scoop out the water once the rains fully subsided. That was a back-breaking task!*
>
> *To compound our problem, there were cracks on the roof. Immediately after the scorching summer, the torrential downpour would make the asbestos roof crack. We had to wait until the*

return of the dry season to repair the roof, because, if we tried to fix the wet roof during the monsoon, it would get damaged again! We would take various precautions and somehow hold out every monsoon.

But 26 July 2005 was different. As usual, it started raining heavily, but my mom was prepared. She had taken all the usual precautions to save the valuables in the house. But we didn't realise the impact that day's rain would have on our lives.

As the intensity of the rain started increasing, water started gushing into our homes. As the water level went up – creeping up to 3 feet – mom started getting worried. My younger brother tried all he could to stop the water from gushing into our house. But after a point, he couldn't control the flow. Neither my dad nor I was at home at that time.

When the situation got worse, my mom and brother decided to save their lives, instead of protecting the lifeless valuables. They managed to jump onto the 13 feet high compound wall with the help of a table and waited there helplessly. Sitting there, my mom saw all our valuables floating out of our home, one by one. The fridge, the gas stove, the bed – everything was gone.

Meanwhile, I was working blissfully at my 2-month old job at a factory. Though I knew it was raining, I didn't realise the intensity of the rain till late in the evening. My mother couldn't inform me either, as we didn't own mobile phones then. Imagine her emotional turmoil – she not only saw our hard-earned possessions float away, but was also not sure if her husband and her son were safe. Neither my father nor I could be contacted. And we couldn't come back home, either, thanks to the rain that had flooded the entire city.

I realised the intensity of the situation, I desperately wanted to be with my family immediately. But my HR team had given strict instructions that we were not to leave the factory premises until the situation improved. Inspite of being worried about the wellbeing of my family, I had to stay put the entire night at the factory. It was one of the worst nights of my life! Even at 5 am the next day, the rains hadn't subsided. But I couldn't stay patient anymore. I sneaked out of the factory without informing my HR manager.

Due to massive flooding, all means of transport had been suspended across the city. The only way to reach home was to walk. I had to walk 25 km to reach home; this took me around 14 hours. Thousands of Mumbaikars walked to their homes that day by forming human chains to save one another from falling into open utility holes or ditches and dying. People who were less impacted by the flood were distributing packaged water and biscuits to make sure others wouldn't go thirsty or hungry.

Finally, when I reached home after a long tiring walk, I saw that the doors were wide open. By now, the water had subsided a little. But, there was nothing left inside the house. In addition, there had been a complete blackout because of a short circuit. I fanatically searched for my family, running helter-skelter. Suddenly I heard my mom's voice calling out for me; she had spotted me. We hugged as if we had never hugged each other before.

That day set us back by ten years in life because everything that we had – including money – got washed away. Our house was layered with 7 or 8 inches of muck. We didn't have cleaners or maids to clean the house for us; we had to do everything ourselves. Fortunately, four of my cousins came and helped us clean up.

That day, I learnt one of the most important lessons of my life. Nature has everything in abundance. It's we who need to know how to use it right for positive impact. For instance, when we have floods, we can solve the problem if we channelise the flood water towards people who don't have water. This thought fuelled my desire to educate myself further and become resourceful. I wanted to help others lead better lives. And that's how I started seeking people who could show me my desired path in life.

I realised that the only gifts I had were the values and the education given to me by my parents. I had neither money nor ancestors' property. Therefore, seeking help to support myself and others became my dominant thought. This overrode any inhibitions I might have had, which could potentially have become a roadblock for my progress. Many people supported me at every step, and my parents didn't leave any stone unturned to get me where I am today. My values (that kept me grounded), my education and my parents' constant support allowed me to grow fearlessly and become highly successful in life."

All I can say is – unbelievable! Starting in the chawls of Mumbai and going on to become a Vice President of a company and the host of LinkedInLocalHyderabad – what a journey it has been for Sagar!

Adversities hit everyone, but how one chooses to deal with them matters the most. Whether you seek help or not matters. I am sure there were other kids in that chawl along with Sagar who couldn't achieve much in life. The difference lay in the approach. In Sagar's words, *"Helplessness is a choice."* One can *choose to be helpless or to be resourceful."*

What would you choose?

> **PAUSE AND REFLECT**
>
> Have you ever faced a setback early in your life? Maybe a physical, emotional or financial problem? If yes, how did you respond to it?
>
> Will your approach change, now that you have read Kuiljeit's, Katherine's and Sagar's stories? I'd love to hear your thoughts.
>
> Feel free to email me at connect@srijatabhatnagar.com

My first conscious encounter with a setback occurred when I was doing my graduation.

I grew up in the sleepy little town of Raiganj in the state of West Bengal in India. I was a bright child in terms of studies. I was keenly interested in learning new concepts, gaining knowledge and applying it, experimenting with ideas and so on. I hated rote learning – sitting with books for long hours without understanding the concepts. I liked to quickly understand a concept and move on to the experiments or the next theory. I disliked definitions, because they had to be written the same way as they appeared in books, and I never understood the need to do that!

I was quick to grasp concepts and apply them in day-to-day life. I had always been among the top five in my class. In my 12th grade board exam, I emerged the district topper. With the new-found happiness and confidence of this achievement, I moved to Kolkata to join one of the best colleges in the state. Till then, I had no idea how a failure or setback tasted. I didn't have a clue about what was in store for me in the coming months.

Life was great! I enjoyed my new college life with new friends, fun and frolic. I was progressing well in my subjects and was upbeat about my performance in the forthcoming exams.

Just two days before the exams, I had a mild fever. Thinking it would be a regular fever, I took a medicine. And the temperature did come down.

On the day of the first exam, sitting in the exam hall and looking at the question paper, I was happy. I knew all the answers pretty well and I started writing them. Within 30 minutes, however, I started feeling cold. At first, my hands began trembling. And then; my whole body started shivering. The shivering was so intense that I had to hold my right hand with my left hand to keep it steady and continue writing. After an hour of this shivering, I gave up. When I informed the invigilator about my situation and asked for his opinion, he asked me if I had written well enough to submit the papers. I responded, "I don't know!"

He asked me to submit the papers, go to the college infirmary, take some medicine and rest. I did as he said. After some time, when I felt a little better, I went to the Principal and requested him to grant me leave on medical grounds – on the promise that I would write the exams as soon as I recovered from my illness. He refused to trust me and said that I would be marked 'failed' if I did not complete the exams this time.

Later that evening, I came to know that I had contracted malaria. That is what had caused the severe shivering and high temperature. The doctor instructed me to take complete rest for a week and to avoid getting stressed. But I knew I had to complete my exams or I would fail. And so, every morning for the next five days, I loaded myself with a heavy dose of medicines and headed to the exam hall.

The effect of the medicines would start wearing off within the first hour of the exam. But I'd continue writing for another 45 mins or an hour, body shaking and hands unsteady. I'd then submit the paper and wait for my friends to accompany me back to the hostel, as I didn't feel strong enough to go alone. But on the third day, I felt so ill that I decided to return to the hostel as soon as possible and sleep. Deciding to not wait for my friends, I went alone. Standing at the bus stop, I suddenly collapsed due to a blackout. Strangers picked me up and dropped me at the hostel.

Next morning, I was back in the exam hall again. When the results of the exam were announced, I was sceptical about my performance, for obvious reasons. And my worst fear came true.

I found out that for the first time in my life, I had failed in an exam. I was devastated, angry and upset. I was blaming myself for this failure. Deep down, I was ashamed of myself.

Don't we all react to exam failures like this? Often, don't we blame ourselves for the results we get?

Some of the people were laughing at me for my result; they taunted me. Only a few who knew what I had gone through during the exams were beside me – consoling me and giving me moral support. How often do we see people who taunt us instead of trying to help?

I stormed out of the college campus, a deluge of inner voices crowding my mind. One said, "What's the point in living with such shame?" Another said, "So what? You have failed, but it is not the end of life." Another voice said, "You are worthless!", while yet another said, "It's alright; you did your best." Yet another said, "Go jump into the Ganges." I was going through an emotional breakdown. Finally, good sense prevailed. I decided to call my father and tell him about this incident.

Dad asked me a few critical questions. "Did you put in your best efforts? Would you have done it differently if you knew how to? You contracting malaria – was it intentional?" My answers were: yes, yes and no respectively. As I answered his questions, I started gaining clarity about the situation. When he asked me to replay the entire episode in my head again, I knew he wanted me to pick up some lessons from this episode. I was so glad I had called him!

I learnt from my first failure, picked up the broken pieces and worked on mending them. Even today, whenever I get into a self-blaming zone, I ask myself the same three questions my father asked me that day.

Learnings

The most important learnings from these stories are:
- ✦ Realise and acknowledge your setbacks, so that you can work on them.
- ✦ Have a dream so big that your setback seems tiny in front of it. Having a massive dream allows you to look for ways to achieve it despite the setback.
- ✦ Be oblivious to society's negative voice and keep your focus on your dream.

- ✦ The mind is a fantastic tool, that, when used right, helps you come out of your setbacks quickly.
- ✦ Success isn't a yardstick that the world should decide for you. You should define your success and achieve it for yourself.
- ✦ When in trouble, seek help from others. There is nothing wrong in it. People love helping others out of a challenge.
- ✦ Your setback is NOT you. Separate yourself from your setback.
- ✦ You shouldn't judge a person's capability by just one isolated incident. There could be more hidden behind that incident.

My father helped me separate myself from my setback. I realised it was not me who was responsible for my failure; it was my situation and circumstances. Could I have changed my condition at that time? No. If I could have changed it, I would have. I did whatever I could to the best of my abilities.

Life lesson: *People are not their setbacks. People survive, whereas setbacks become a thing of the past.*

PAUSE AND REFLECT

I invite you to ask yourself the following questions regarding a serious challenge you faced:

1. Did you put in your best efforts prior to it?
2. Would you have done anything differently if you knew better? If yes, what?
3. Was this setback intentional? Or could you have controlled the situation?

Your answers will surely give you a lot of clarity. You will not only be able to evaluate your setback objectively, but will also be able to handle the next tough situation you face better.

✦✦✦

In the next chapter, we will examine a few serious professional setbacks people have gone through in their lives. Did you apply for your dream job and get rejected? Did you miss a significant promotion? Or, were you ever laid off from your job? Did someone backstab you, because of which you lost something meaningful at work?

How did you deal with the situation? What is the first thing you thought or did? Write down your response on a sheet of paper before you read the next chapter. Be honest with your answers; they are only for your reference. If you can't be honest with yourself, how can you expect to benefit from this exercise?

CHAPTER 2

Workplace Woes

If you are thinking, "Oh, come on! Leaders and professional setbacks? Just not possible!", let me burst that bubble right away.

ROGER CHEETHAM

Roger Cheetham (https://www.linkedin.com/in/roger-cheetham-371576164/) is a multi-award winning international speaker, resilience specialist and author from the United Kingdom. He also happens to be a murder attempt survivor. Today, he believes that the horrific, life-threatening experience (the murder attempt, about which we will read in a subsequent chapter) is one of the best things that happened in his life. Instead of seeing it as an experience that happened *to* him, he thinks it happened *for* him. Not just for *him*, but for the thousands of people that he inspires today. Using his own story, Roger delivers an inspiring message of resilience at his talks and workshops around the world.

Let's hear from Roger about a serious professional setback he faced early on in his career:

> "I had gone for an interview for the job of my dreams, but was told that I didn't have the confidence to fit that employer's needs. I was just 18 years old and fresh out of college. I was not only disappointed that I didn't qualify for the job, but also shattered to hear that I was seen to be under-confident.
>
> Though I was dejected, I gathered the courage to ask them what exactly was wrong. And they gladly gave me honest feedback, pointing out that I didn't show confidence while answering the questions. It was everything – from my posture to the initial handshake and various other non-verbal and verbal things that I can't recall now, as it happened to me over 30 years ago.
>
> After receiving detailed feedback, I decided to work on myself instead of wallowing in self-pity. Around six months later, I came to know that the person who had taken on the role I had applied for didn't work there anymore. Incidentally, I was called for a re-interview because, except for my under-confidence, they were impressed with everything else about me. Today, I am pleased to say that, on that second occasion, I grabbed the job. From among 14 applicants, I was the chosen one. And I went on to work for this company for more than 12 years!"

What worked in Roger's favour was his approach to tackling the setback: he took the rejection positively, listened to the feedback and worked hard on the issues that were pointed out, instead of retorting to a blame game or moping around in self-pity.

Contrast this with the common attitude we see around us. Most people do nothing about the feedback given to them; they hate being criticised and keep blaming everything around them for their setbacks. It sometimes feels as if they love to stay in that self-pity zone; they start *liking* the pain.

LAUREN POWERS

Lauren Powers (http://www.laurenpowers.com/) is a ten-time heavyweight bodybuilding champion, author, entrepreneur, model and actor. She is the founder of the Lauren Powers Classic and Powers Fitness Events in the USA. Powers Fitness Events represents Team USA in fitness and bodybuilding for men and women. Apart from authoring two books 'Beneath the Muscle' and 'Unleash Your Inner Champion', Lauren is an award-winning international speaker on cinema and media. She has judged many bodybuilding events in the USA and throughout the world. She has been featured in numerous Hollywood films, documentaries and television shows. She has worked with Nick Jonas, Jennifer Hudson, Iggy Azalea, Jennifer Lopez and many other celebrities in Hollywood.

Lauren has always represented the underdog and is a passionate spokesperson for people who are 'different'. She lives by the motto, "It's the hard that makes it good; if it were easy, everyone would do it."

She too had her share of professional challenges early in her career. Here, she talks about one of them:

> "At the beginning of my career, I wanted to be a firefighter. That was my dream job. Being an adventurous girl, I thought firefighting would be the best career choice for me, as I believed in helping others. I enthusiastically went to the National Fire Academy (NFA) in the US for the firefighters' training. I trained sincerely for more than a year and joined the organisation. But, in the end, I landed up with a lawsuit, because my colleagues – especially the men – didn't want a woman on the job. That's why they ganged up to ensure that I was one of the three women that did not get promoted.
>
> It was devastating at that time. I was distraught, because I had put in a humongous amount of effort for a year and a half through depositions, working on improving my physical fitness, etc. And here, my fellow firefighters didn't even want to work with me! When you are risking your life for your work, you need your team to support you, especially in high-risk jobs like firefighting. I was highly disappointed and deeply hurt.
>
> Eventually, I realised there was no need to fight a lost battle. I gave up firefighting and turned towards other open doors. I was in the process of building my body because of the strict physical agility guidelines of the NFA; so I already had an inclination towards fitness. This inclination only got stronger post this unfortunate event. And thanks to my bodybuilding, I got discovered in Las Vegas. I was on TV and became a national celebrity almost overnight! That's how my journey as a fitness icon and actor started.

"Looking back now, I feel my firefighting colleagues did me the biggest favour of all, because I wouldn't be who I am today if they hadn't behaved the way they did. Today, I am a famous fitness icon and a role model. All the exciting things that I get to do – TV, radio, commercials, film, music videos, etc. – wouldn't have been possible otherwise. I have a beautiful life today because of the discrimination I faced years ago."

Now I thank them, I bless them, I wave at them when I drive by. Thanks to that incident, I am living up my life! My focus on day-to-day life has completely shifted; now I let things flow the way they're supposed to, without force-fitting anything. Today, I know if something has to happen, it will happen, and nothing can be forced."

Lauren's story tells us to be grateful for every situation life presents us with, even if it is a challenging one. Because that setback can become the turning point of our life. We may not realise it initially and may get bogged down by the incident. But later, we will understand how that setback helped in our growth and success. Provided, of course, that we are ready to see the setback from an objective point of view, learn from it and apply the learnings to our life.

It's important to accept things that are beyond our control and let them take their course, without losing the big picture.

DIAZ RICHARDS

Diaz Richards (https://www.linkedin.com/in/diaz-richards-980b4743/) is an award-winning international speaker and the founder of 'Journey Back to Source'. She grew up on a tiny island in the Caribbean. Today, she is settled in the UK and plays an essential role in the shift of humanity's consciousness. Her vision is to create global and universal peace by reawakening humanity to its God-essence. To accomplish this, she uses simple techniques to shift the mindset of individuals, so that they can start achieving a grander version of who they are at their core. As a child, she faced many challenges. She believes those challenges were instrumental in shaping who she is today.

However, Diaz didn't start her professional life as a speaker. She did her share of meandering, before finally tapping into her ultimate passion. And in that process, she had to go through a few professional challenges that many of you will be able to relate with. How she chose to deal with such an experience can guide a lot of others who put up with crap at the workplace.

> Diaz says, "In 2005, I was working with a property management firm in the UK. The head of the team, Reuben Davidson, was known to be a Casanova and he called all his girl team members 'Reuben's Girls' – as if they were Charlie's Angels! Some of these 'Reuben's Girls' formed his special team and gave him sexual pleasures. In return, these girls would get a good bonus, expensive gifts, the chance to go out with him and so on. Reuben would brag about this to other senior colleagues.
>
> I refused to play this game with him. My conscience didn't allow me to give in to this. My body is my temple. Also, my philosophy is that my professional life and my personal life are separate. Therefore, I didn't fit into Reuben's team. In return, he would treat me differently from other team members. Where others would get thousands of pounds as bonus for Christmas, I would get just 200 pounds. Everyone would get Christmas gifts, but I wouldn't. I would be excluded from team-building exercises and other team outings, too.
>
> He tried putting pressure on me indirectly and sometimes directly, calling me a lousy team player and the 'worst performer'.

He challenged me by writing a horrible performance review about my work to my super boss, saying I was not a team player and that I sucked at my job. That was the final nail in the coffin.

Reuben and I fought. I confronted him, asking if he could justify my performance review. I challenged him to provide examples of incidents where I hadn't been a team player. Refusing to accept his crap, I wrote to the CEO of the company. The CEO called a meeting, where he read my performance review in front of Reuben and myself. I told the CEO that Reuben hadn't justified any of his remarks about me. I made sure I stood my ground, saying, 'Is this because I do not fit into the role of your 'Reuben's Girls'? I won't play your dirty games, nor will I sit here and accept all your false derogatory remarks.' I requested the CEO to assign me to a different team, which he obliged. This hurt Reuben's big ego and, taking undue advantage of his influential position, he made me leave the company eventually.

Fortunately, I was single at that time. Therefore, this incident didn't affect me much, financially. I told myself, 'You are worthy Diaz; you are a well-educated, intelligent girl. You have professional accolades. You will find another job.' It didn't make sense for me to fight for that shitty job anyway; so I went ahead and signed up with various job portals and head hunters. And within a few weeks, I got another job!

The property management field in the UK is a close-knit one. And so, I would meet Reuben somewhere or the other. And he would try to create a misunderstanding between my new bosses and me. But they were wise; they knew the truth. They knew I was professional, I performed well and that clients were happy with me. Hence, they chose to ignore his nuisance.

My philosophy in life is that we can go through any shitty experience in life. Whether we want to be a victim or a victor is our choice. I believe we ourselves are the architects of our lives. Thoughts makes people what they are. For instance, if I tell myself, 'I am a failure', failure is what I am going to manifest. And so, be careful about your thoughts, and only think of what you truly want to manifest."

It is fascinating to know the different kinds of challenges people face at their workplaces. It is unfortunate to see such things happening in professional spaces all over the world. The only consolation is that we have examples of leaders who chose to deal with them in ways that helped them move forward.

The way Diaz stood up to the unacceptable behaviour of her boss is something to learn from. It's essential to raise your voice and hold your ground firmly when you must. At the same time, know that you cannot control others' behaviour; all you can do is to decide how to respond to it. What happened to Diaz's lousy boss is unimportant, but what *she* did to change her crappy situation is the key point.

> **PAUSE AND REFLECT**
>
> Are you facing a setback at your workplace or have you faced one before? How are you dealing/did you deal with it?
>
> Do you think Roger, Lauren or Diaz's story can help you deal with your professional setback in a more productive way?
>
> Would you like to explore more techniques to deal with your professional setbacks?
>
> Write to me at connect@srijatabhatnagar.com and I will be happy to respond with my thoughts.

I have had multiple professional setbacks, too. The most prominent of them occurred when I was working in one of the largest multinational sports companies in the world.

It was a dream job, and I was super happy at my workplace. I enjoyed the role; my team and my boss were good, too. My boss knew our strengths and weaknesses well. She knew how to utilise our strengths not only for the company's benefit but also to help us grow quickly. Those in our team were the rockstars of the company – most approachable, highly responsive and the smartest. We were the favourites of all the other departments.

I grabbed three promotions in three consecutive years! I rose quickly, not only in designation but also in terms of responsibilities. Life was good. Meanwhile, I discovered that I was pregnant – something that made me even happier! Though I had a troubled pregnancy, I wanted to keep working through it. And that's what I did – until the final moments, I was working and managing different projects efficiently.

Post-delivery, I decided to take a maternity break of 6 months, as allowed by the company. Though I was on a break, I stayed in touch with my work. I attended relevant meetings and helped with the deliverables from home, once in a while.

Meanwhile, my boss resigned. And the company had changed its strategic direction, which I was partially aware of. When I returned to office, I went through a series of trainings to align myself with the new vision and mission of the company. I was coping well in this new environment, learning quickly and implementing at the same time. During this time, a new boss joined. All of us knew she wasn't as efficient as the earlier one, but we didn't care much about it, because we knew our responsibilities well. The more we started working with her, the more we realised that she was not only inefficient but also unethical. She would take credit for all our hard work, but would blame us if something went wrong. Once, she fired one of my colleagues for a mistake he didn't commit – to hide her own inefficiency.

All of us were increasingly getting frustrated, but we tolerated it for a few months. Then came the time for the performance appraisal. Even in my worst nightmare, I had never imagined that I would be demoted!

Yes, I was demoted for no reason. That's when I lost it! I went up to my boss and sought an explanation. She couldn't even look me in the eye. Instead, she gave several lame excuses for her wrong action.

Also, she told me not to discuss my appraisal with other colleagues. I couldn't take this injustice. When I shared the details of my appraisal with my colleagues, including business heads, everyone was shocked! But my boss refused to budge, fearing that she will get a bad name from the management for this error. Instead, she had the gall to ask me to accept the demotion with grace.

I was furious; I knew I had to do something. I couldn't fall prey to someone else's stupid whims and fancies. And so, I wrote a stinker to the entire top management, including the India CEO, the global CEO, the Chairman, other business heads and a few directors on the board. Also, I decided I wouldn't work for a boss like this – someone who manipulates people for their gain and treats team members as pawns who will serve their secret agenda. I started applying for other jobs and moved out of that company in a month.

A couple of months later, I came to know that my ex-boss had been fired from the company due to disciplinary issues and incompetence.

Learnings

People see many kinds of challenges in professional spaces. What Roger, Lauren, Diaz and I did when faced with such setbacks offers significant lessons. Let me summarise the key learnings for you:

- Taking feedback from setbacks and sincerely working on it is the way to improve yourself.
- It is essential to let go of things that aren't meant to work and turn towards things that **will** work.
- It is essential to raise your voice and stick to your guns when required.
- Listen to your inner-consciousness, instead of listening to the noise outside.
- It's not YOU; it's the situation and the environment. Take quick action to change the situation or the environment you are in, as applicable.

+ People never get away with wrongdoings, unless you let them. The choice is yours. Will you stay quiet or will you raise your voice and take action?

When I look back today, I know that the incident I narrated happened for my good, because I needed that jolt to pursue my dream of becoming an entrepreneur. I was getting too comfortable at my workplace and had forgotten my dream. This jolt put me in a position of discomfort, thereby making sure that I pursued my dreams eventually.

Life lesson: *The world may throw different kinds of setbacks at us. How we respond to them is our choice.*

I chose to respond to the setback in a manner that didn't create a layer of baggage in my mind. And it helped me grow in the right direction.

> **PAUSE AND REFLECT**
>
> I invite you to introspect about your professional challenges – past and present.
>
> - Each time you were faced with a professional roadblock or problem, did you put in sincere efforts to overcome it? Is something bothering you about any setback even now? If yes, what is it?
>
> - Do/did you have control over the situation? If yes, what can you do about it/what did you do about it?
>
> - Is/was the outcome the best you deserved? If your answer is no, what actions did you take/are you taking to change your reality for the better?
>
> Your honest introspection will help you not only find ways to come out of your sticky situation, but also to achieve your dreams.

✦ ✦ ✦

We will talk about another fragile topic in the next chapter – failed romantic relationships. At least 95% of the people I meet or work with have had a failed romantic relationship. And the vast majority of people believe that once they have experienced *'heartbreak'*, it's impossible to find true love again!

What do **you** believe about finding true love? Do you think it is a beautiful experience or do you feel it is only for losers? Do you get excited about finding your soulmate or do you get anxious and disappointed? Does your heart quiver with fear the moment you think of dating someone or are you enthusiastic about it?

Jot down your thoughts before you flip this page.

CHAPTER 3

The Broken Heart Syndrome

When **Diaz Richards,** the award-winning international speaker, mentor and founder of 'Journey Back to Source' told me about her love failures, I had goosebumps! It felt as if the Universe had put her through different kinds of stringent tests to prepare her for bigger things in life. Diaz says,

> *"I grew up in the Caribbean, where there is an open culture when it comes to love, relationships and sex education; it was not taboo. Therefore, I have had a few boyfriends. Whether I loved them or not is another question. My grandmom would always tell us, 'Children, only cockroaches don't have boyfriends. Have boyfriends, but bring them home. Let us meet them, because one day, they might become your family'. Even though I had boyfriends, I was never in a sexual relationship until I was 21 years old. I believed my body is my temple, and it was my choice who to give it to.*
>
> *Marvin was the first man I truly loved. I always had a special bond with him. He was 25 years older than me, but when we met, I felt as if I was meeting a part of my soul. He knew that, as well. Our relationship was so deep, that silence was enough to express our connection; we didn't need a sexual encounter to form that connection. Unlike me, he belonged to a wealthy and influential family. Though I knew I was the first woman he loved truly, I had to let him go. I had to leave the island to explore my professional ambitions abroad. And he couldn't come with me because of his family duties. It was a complicated relationship,*

> but it was the one where I experienced true love. That's why he will always be in my happy memories.
>
> It took me five long years to get him out of my system. I would keep thinking about him, dwelling in his thoughts. Eventually, I decided to delve into my spiritual self. I read a lot of self-help books, did affirmations and dated other men, so that I could keep my mind off Marvin. But inside, my heart was aching terribly. Even though we had broken up, my heart was still with him.
>
> Even today, I feel a strange attachment towards him, inspite of knowing that nothing is possible between us now. It's been many years; I am married and have a beautiful daughter. Unfortunately, my marriage of 12 years will soon end, because I have asked for a divorce. My husband and I have stopped growing together."

My heart goes out to Diaz and all others who found true love, but for whom it didn't culminate in a life-long relationship. Some relationships are meant to be that way. They don't have a conclusion or result. They are meant to be stored away in a corner of your heart. You feel great about the time you spent together and let it be.

In this book, I also want to highlight setbacks of a personal nature that people go through, and that change their entire belief system forever. Belief systems don't form only in our professional lives; they are shaped by *every* experience and situation we go through. Therefore, an essential aspect of setback leadership is to look into your personal experiences and see what you can infer from them.

Love setback is one such substantial setback. It puts unwanted limiting beliefs into people's minds regarding themselves and their capabilities. It stalls their free growth in more than one way. One of my coaching clients came up to me and said, *"I am terrible with women. Whoever I love rejects me. There must be something fundamentally wrong with me."* It took me months to change his belief about himself, especially around rejections.

What about leaders? Even they go through crazy heartbreaks. They may not be walking around with those heartbreaks on their sleeves; but like anybody else, they have been through such experiences, too.

I know another person like Diaz, who found true love, and yet, couldn't take it forward to a logical conclusion. No matter how much we plan our lives, sometimes the Universe's plan prevails.

We already got a glimpse of **Sagar Amlani**'s early major setback on a rainy day in Mumbai in 2005. That incident set the path for him. He became earnest about studying and acquiring knowledge. But when it came to love, the Universe had other plans for him. Sagar recalls,

"In college, there was a girl who claimed to be madly in love with me; so much so that she started journaling about me daily. She started writing down what I wore to college, what I said in class and how she liked every action of mine, sitting right behind me. I was blissfully unaware of all this. It was after three months, when she proposed to me with a 90-page book saying she was in love with me and wanted to marry me, that I realised what was going on. I wasn't in a frame of mind to understand her feelings, leave alone agree to marry her. I had joined college to study, do well in life and eventually end my parents' miseries. Distractions like relationships were not for me.

I told her to ignore this infatuation and concentrate on studies. Instead, she threatened that she would commit suicide if I didn't accept her proposal. I was scared – because if someone died in my name and I were accused of it, then not only I, but my family too would be in trouble. Fortunately, I had a soul sister in college. Knowing that only a girl could counsel another girl, I called my soul sister immediately and narrated my plight. I arranged a meeting between her, the other girl and me. The girl who had proposed to me started crying and blaming me for revealing her secrets to others. She said she felt humiliated. Eventually, my soul sister took her to the girls' hostel and talked her out of it. The girl started behaving normally with me from the next day, and I heaved a sigh of relief.

I thought this episode ended there, and we all went on with our lives. I graduated and started working in Mumbai. One day, I received a call from a college junior of mine. She was coming to Mumbai for her summer internship. She wanted to meet me, yet was hesitant. When I asked her about her hesitation, she accused me of taking advantage of that other girl (who had been infatuated with me), physically and mentally. She said that she had always seen me as a person of high integrity and ethics; so, this had come as a nasty surprise to her. She said she wanted to meet me and confront me for all my misdeeds!

My conscience was pure; that's why I wasn't afraid of facing her. We met and ended up talking for more than 5 hours! After hearing my side of the story in detail and getting it validated by my soul sister, she apologised to me profusely. That day, we became close. We started talking to each other – often for hours together – and came to share a close bond. I know that was the first time both of us felt the love between us.

After her summer internship, she moved back to her college. Fortunately, the city where her college was located was not very far from Mumbai, where I was living. I therefore started visiting her over weekends. Our attachment grew stronger, day by day. We had a platonic relationship, where just the presence of each was enough to make the other happy. Even holding hands felt sacred.

Then came the day of her graduation. She invited me to be a part of her celebrations. I had no clue that even her father was going to be present there. Nor did I know that he knew about our relationship.

After spending two days together, seeing the respect I commanded from students, my professors' affection for me, the way I treated people and vice versa, and how his daughter adored me, uncle was visibly impressed. But on the day he was to return to his hometown, I found him crying in the garden. When I enquired, he started apologising to me. He said that though he knew I was the right man for his daughter and would like her to marry me, he couldn't let that happen. On enquiring further, he said, 'If I let both of you get married, my wife will commit suicide on the day of the wedding. She has sworn to me on this point'.

For a few minutes, I was in shock! Eventually collecting my thoughts and comforting uncle, I said, 'I have lived 23 years of life without your daughter; I will manage to live the rest of my life, too. I don't want to get married at the cost of someone's life. Also, there is no point getting married without the blessings of elders'. Although I managed to say this to show maturity, strength and integrity, reality set in soon – I was going to lose her forever! I just couldn't control my emotions. I went to my soul sister's place and wept continuously for more than two days. At the same time, my girlfriend was shattered, as well.

After I returned to Mumbai, I punished myself by not eating for 21 days. I would leave home in the morning before breakfast, roam around the city aimlessly and return home late at night, after dinnertime. And then one day, my mom caught me. When she probed a little, I broke down. I shared my pain with her, pouring my heart out. She didn't console me much; she said only one thing, 'Whatever happens always happens for the good. Wait a few years. You will know why I said this.'

To me, it all seemed too preachy at that time. But today, when I look back, I know mom was right. It was exhausting and painful; it took time for me to get my girlfriend out of my system, especially since neither of us had been at fault. For the next few years, I buried myself in books and studies. I spent time in introspecting and in acknowledging my emotions.

Doing that has helped me live a guilt-free life today. Just imagine – I am still friends with that girl. She has a doting husband and I have an amazing wife. Mansi is the best person I could ever get married to. She is grounded in her values. In every sense, she is truly my better half. She knows me and understands me better than I do myself. I am blessed to have her in my life."

Both Diaz and Sagar chose to let go of their soulmates for different reasons, though they could've done otherwise. I see the youth of today doing just the opposite – fleeing with their partners or forcing their families to accept their partners, thereby creating an atmosphere of hatred and distrust.

At the same time, I also see a lot of families put unnecessary pressure on their children to make them succumb to their (the families') choice. They emotionally blackmail their children with dire consequences.

Both these approaches aren't healthy, either for the couple or the family. Couples should understand that though they may choose to be together without the family's approval, they may not be able to lead a happy life forever. There could be guilt, remorse and other unproductive emotions lingering. And families should understand that marriage isn't about status or community; it's about the compatibility of two people who need to live together happily. It is essential to have mutual respect and love. They should stop throwing their children into the lifelong fire of a loveless or respectless marriage.

> **PAUSE AND REFLECT**
>
> Have you ever failed in love? Did you get rejected or go through one-sided love? Were you forced to marry someone you didn't love or respect? How has your life shaped up due to these incidents?
>
> Are you struggling to come out of a relationship setback and need help? Feel free to write to me at connect@srijatabhatnagar.com

I have been through love failures, too. From severe eve-teasing in early teenage to roadside Romeos making my life hell; finding it confusing to spot the difference between thrill, infatuation and real love; heartbreaks, rejections, double-crosses, humiliation and self-realisation – you name it, and I have experienced it. It was extremely challenging to grow up freely as a girl in a small town in West Bengal, India.

Today, I realise that those experiences have made me the way I am. They helped me prepare myself for more significant challenges in life. Thanks to these experiences, I have become a better person when it comes to love.

I have heard many times from my fellow relationship experts that it is difficult to love others when you don't know how to love yourself. I completely agree with this, because that's precisely what I experienced, too.

My first serious break-up happened at the age of 20. I was already failing in my studies, when my boyfriend decided to break up with me. All of a sudden, he started avoiding me. This seemed very unusual to me; I couldn't figure out what was going on. Why was he behaving so strangely? It was he who had proposed to me and coaxed me for long. He had been the one who made sure that our mutual friends convinced me about his seriousness before I had agreed to explore this relationship. This boy who had been so keen about our relationship – how could he decide to call it quits suddenly? This was a rude shock to me!

I have always believed that if I am committed to someone, I must give my best. And so, I did my best to understand his disproportionately strange behaviour. Generally, people start blaming either others or themselves for the misery they undergo. And my upbringing had taught me to look within and check what *I* had done wrong. But the more I looked within, the more disappointed I became. There were no answers, only questions. During this quest to find answers, a mutual friend saw my agony and let out a shocking secret.

Apparently, my so-called boyfriend and some of our other mutual friends had had a challenge going between them. If he could convince me to accept his proposal, he would win the challenge. It had just been a game for them. I was mad; but still, I wanted to hear the truth from my boyfriend. What followed was a game of 'hide and seek' between him and me. I would wish to get some time alone with him, and he would give me several excuses for not meeting me. During this incident, I learnt a vital aspect of human behaviour.

> **When people know they are guilty, they avoid confrontation. They avoid talking to the person they have hurt.**

This made me even more desperate to talk to him; I was losing patience (these days, I know when someone is avoiding me, when someone should be left alone and when I should move on. But back then, it was different). When I finally confronted him, he confessed that he had indeed been playing a game with me. Erupting like a volcano of anger in front of the entire college, I slapped him. People had to separate me forcibly, because I was beating him up!

In many ways, our society is so toxic for everybody, both boys and girls. Often, a boy decides to show off his masculinity by playing with a girl's heart and his friends cheer him along. Even today, it is so easy for some men to treat women as objects of entertainment, to prove their machismo. They start stalking them on social media and send them weird proposals, expecting them (the girls) to jump at them excitedly. All I can say to such men is, GROW UP!

The impact of my heartbreak and humiliation was so bad, that I fell ill immediately. I had a sudden high fever and was bedridden for a week. Deep inside, I was hurting; I felt like a toy that anyone could play with. I was angry with myself for not judging the boy's intentions right. But I couldn't share my anguish with anyone. Sharing it with my family was out of the question; we were never taught to share such matters with our families. And telling my friends would make me feel even worse, I thought. I felt violated, betrayed, disgusted and utterly unhappy with myself.

'Every cloud has a silver lining' goes the famous proverb. While self-sabotaging, I realised that I was crying for someone who didn't deserve my love. How could it be my fault if *his* intentions were wrong? After I asked myself this question, I got up from bed, transformed; a new version of me was born that day. I became fiercely focused on my studies and career, just like Diaz and Sagar. I drowned myself in books. But there was a cost to this transformation – I became a man-hater, turning into a rude, ruthless, unkind and arrogant human being, who hated every man who came her way.

Life moved on. I achieved whatever I wanted to, from the education point of view. I cleared CAT (one of the toughest and most competitive entrance exams in India for management courses) and secured a seat in MBA in a college in Chennai. I was excited to explore new pastures, a new place and new learnings. In Chennai, life settled into another groove. I started adjusting well to the new college, my new friends and my new habitat. I was enjoying my classes and was happy in my new little world. But the bitter memories would haunt me whenever a boy would advance with the intention of a romantic link-up. I would become aggressive and insult him. I had created an invisible protective fence around me, and no man was allowed inside that fence. My arrogance and anger earned me the name 'The Royal Bengal Tigress'.

My second break-up happened at the age of 23. Someone managed to penetrate my invisible shield of protection and reach my heart. A tall, fair, handsome and polite boy, who seemed to respect girls not because they were girls, but because they were human beings, captured my heart slowly. His respectful conversations, friendly smiles, eagerness to see me happy and his friendly jokes started melting my shield. I was getting drawn towards him. He grew into me and in one of my weakest moments, settled into my heart. Again, I was completely serious about this relationship and made sure he knew it from Day One.

He agreed to it initially. But after a couple of months, he started behaving strangely – avoiding my calls and requests to meet. He would spend time with my friends, but would ignore me. By now, I knew what these actions meant. I waited for about a month for him to return to me, then gave up. I told myself that there was no point going after someone who didn't adore me, for whom I was not a priority and who would not hesitate to hurt me. I decided it was best to leave him alone.

This time, I was far steadier and handled the situation with much more maturity than earlier. I started ignoring my boyfriend. I was indifferent about his appearance and disappearance among our group of friends. Life moved on, and I learnt my lessons yet again.

Relationships are never static. First, they are seeded. Then, we water them regularly, take care of them, give them enough sunshine and shade – and then, they sprout. Even after they sprout, we need to keep nurturing them. Only then do they grow into lush green plants. There is absolutely nothing called 'love at first sight'. Movies often portray an over-simplified version of love and romance. One should take time to trust and to get involved with a person romantically.

I have seen both my so-called ex-boyfriends guilt-ridden, just because they were not open about their intentions and the expected outcome from the relationship. There is no harm in getting into a casual relationship, as long as both partners agree to it. If one partner is serious about the relationship but the other is casual about it, there is a problem. The committed person goes through a heartbreak invariably, whereas the person looking for a casual link-up may also go through a guilt trip and have behavioural issues, eventually.

Learnings

Today, when I coach people, I tell them to follow these guidelines while exploring a romantic relationship with someone:

- ✦ Let your partner know your true intentions. From the beginning, be open about the outcome you expect from the relationship.
- ✦ Respect your partner and his/her choices, plans and desired results.
- ✦ Never deceive your partner; have an open conversation when things aren't going smoothly.
- ✦ Don't ignore it when things are complicated or confusing. Face it and be open about your thoughts and feelings.
- ✦ Understand the non-verbal signs to gauge the interest levels of the other person. (*I made the mistake of pursuing someone who wasn't interested in me and waited for him for a long time; simply because I wanted to have a conversation with him. If I had understood his non-verbal cues, I would have seen that he wanted to avoid exactly that! Avoid this mistake, and you will avoid hurting yourself more. Observe and feel the non-verbal cues.*)
- ✦ Know that all relationships are not meant to have a happy or finite conclusion. It is best to let some relationships go.
- ✦ Never pursue a relationship forcefully, especially when either your partner or your family is resisting it. Solve the issue; don't let it fester.
- ✦ Families should let their children choose their partner freely, knowing that their happiness lies in the happiness of their children.

Life lesson: ***Just because you have had a few bad experiences, the whole world is not bad. Love will find its way to you when you are ready to receive it.***

Just like *I* found real love, even after two relationships that had gone wrong. I found love in a sensitive man who planted the seed well, watered it right, allowed it to sprout, nurtured it and held it close. And love grew and flourished in no time!

A few months after my second break-up, I started getting friendly with a boy from my batch in college. He was one of the most popular boys in class. A polite, calm, sensible and soft-spoken person, Aneesh was adored by everyone. As destiny would have it, we were partners in a project. Naturally, our interactions increased. Eventually, we started hanging out together more and got to know each other better. He had had a break-up around the same time, too; a fact that helped us bond well. Slowly, we became good friends, then best friends and eventually, inseparable friends. Neither of us realised precisely when love crept into our hearts.

I think it was when I went for a blind date with someone else (on the insistence of another friend) that I realised there was something more than friendship between Aneesh and me. That night, Aneesh was so worried about my safety (because I had stayed out late for the blind date) that he called me and started scolding me for my 'irresponsible behaviour'. One thing led to another, and during that conversation, I realised we had unique feelings for each other.

As I write this book 16 years later, I am still exploring love and life with him. We are each other's best friend, critic, philosopher and guide; and yes, a partner in the adventure called life.

I believe it is essential to explore love wholeheartedly, with an open mind. Heartbreaks will come and go; you must learn from them and make yourself ready to receive love again. Unless you are ready, you will not receive the love you are looking for.

Get rid of your fear of setbacks and freely explore love. And it is bound to happen!

✦✦✦

The next chapter will see us talk about how society sometimes creates a challenging environment and presents us with human-made setbacks, primarily because of preconceived notions of what is 'normal' and what is not.

What was the craziest thing society ever told you? Have you been called a misfit or felt like you were one?

The question remains – who should decide if something is 'normal' or not and in what context?

CHAPTER 4

Square Peg in a Round Hole

You know what, misfits are the reason the world sees innovation. Where everyone else sees a problem, misfits ask why it is a problem. They ask, "What can I do to solve it?"

Sir Isaac Newton was a misfit, too. If he had not asked why the apple *fell* from the tree instead of going up, we would have never known about gravity! I love meeting misfits, as they are the ones who open the doors to possibilities. They are the ones who ask 'WHY NOT?' instead of asking 'WHY?'

Diaz Richards' childhood experience gives us an extraordinary peek into the life of a misfit. Not just society, but even her mother abused the child Diaz – only because she didn't fit into society's definition of 'normal'.

> *"From the age of six or seven, I was the subject to a lot of physical abuse by my mother for many years. She was convinced that I was the devil's child because of my personality. She would ask me, 'Why are you so weird, Diaz? Why are you so different? You are crazy. Why can't you be like other kids?'*
>
> *This was because I used to regularly have encounters with various other-worldly beings on their astral or spiritual journey. I would have a sudden blackout, where my legs would get paralysed temporarily. All of a sudden, I would collapse on the ground. I would hear high pitched sounds and would see colours in shades of dark blue, pink, indigo and purple. I would feel as if I were falling into an abyss of nothingness. Whenever I had such an episode of spiritual experience, my friends would just run*

away from me, leaving me on the ground, paralysed and seeking help. But no one would be there to help me.

I couldn't explain these experiences to my mother or my family. For one, I didn't know how to articulate them correctly. And secondly, they had already dubbed me weird and different; I didn't want to worsen my plight by telling them about each new experience. Imagine a seven-year-old kid going through such experiences, where she is not able to understand what's going on or who to seek help from to understand these encounters.

I started experiencing these encounters when I was about four years old. By the time I was six or seven years old, I had had my Conscious Spiritual Awakening, wherein I had begun asking about the meaning of life and going on a search to find the answers.

I would know things about my teachers that my parents thought I shouldn't know or say, being a child. I remember one particular teacher, Mrs Wilkinson. I saw her as being very unbalanced and asked her why her husband was abusing her. She freaked out and complained to my Aunt Denise, who was also a teacher at the same school. Aunt Denise came home and announced the incident to the rest of the family. Each such incident resulted in my getting beaten up by my mother. She was convinced that I was demonically possessed. And so, she would curse me saying, 'You are the devil's child! You know what? I am going to beat the devil out of you.' And she would start beating me with whatever came her way – even a leather strap or twigs. If nothing else, she would beat me with her hand. Once, I was held up by one leg and kept dangling in mid-air like a rag-doll, while my mother beat me black and blue.

> "Every time I think of my mother, all I can remember is being subject to tremendous physical and mental abuse. She would put me down saying, 'You are a dunce (dumb person)'. I started believing that I was indeed a dunce. Although I was an intelligent, active, bubbly and enthusiastic child, each time my mother was around, I would shut down and under-perform."

My tiny body and young mind were under a lot of stress. Finally, I rebelled. I revolted and made a pact with God. That day onwards, I started calling God my mom and dad. 'I am God's Child', I'd say. Eventually, my mom decided to emigrate and left me with my grandparents. That was the first time I felt liberated."

When I heard Diaz narrate this, I had goosebumps. I have heard of society rebuking someone for being 'abnormal' before, but Diaz's story is unprecedented! Honestly, I can't even imagine what little Diaz would've been through, all those years!

At the same time, I am amazed at the way she left those sufferings behind to walk in the path of peace, love and confidence. Her story teaches us the lesson that even if no one comes to our rescue, we'd better pull up our socks and fight for ourselves. Ultimately, we are our best cheerleaders or worst critiques. The choice is ours, regarding which of these roles we want to play.

NIKHIL CHAUDHARY

Sometimes, society starts alienating people when they fail or go through a tough situation in life. Something similar happened to **Nikhil Chaudhary** (https://www.nikhilchaudhary.com/). Nikhil is an international speaker from India and an expert in reversing diseases like diabetes, liver problems, cholesterol, heart diseases and terminal cases of cancer using diet. He has had case studies published in international journals and has presented papers at conferences. A board member of the prestigious Professional Speakers Association of India (PSAI), Nikhil has clients from over two dozen countries. He has been featured in many Indian newspapers (such as Times of India, New Indian Express, Deccan Chronicle and others). Nikhil's mission is to spread awareness of the concept "food is medicine". This is how he narrates his story:

> *"Coming from a business background, my entire clan knows how to do business and make a lot of money. So, if an individual is not wealthy or is unable to make money, he is generally looked down upon and neglected. When I failed in my businesses multiple times and gave up the desire to make money due to a significant personal setback for the most prolonged period, my community behaved as if I had no capability. My desire to live life had vanished due to that setback, and the only two reasons I survived the harsh realities of life were my mom and my wife.*

"Helping people gave me immense happiness, and hence, my entire focus shifted to assisting people in reversing their diseases using my knowledge of diet and nutrition."

> *My education in biotechnology and my understanding of biochemistry, microbiology, etc. helped me gain knowledge about nutrition and health. Eventually, I learnt that rather than genetics, diet and lifestyle choices determine the diseases a person attracts. Therefore, preventing diseases is a conscious choice. However, many people don't realise this. I did intensive*

research and using my knowledge, began reversing common lifestyle diseases. In time, I started treating even terminal stage cancer through diet.

By then, I had given up on the money-making race. I used to spend most of my time in social work, helping people recover from their bad health. I used to do it without much monetary gain. I wasn't making a lot of money, because I was not interested in it. I had just enough money to run the house.

At that time, my clan, my community and in fact, almost everyone felt I was a loser. Though no one disrespected me or said anything to my face, I could always sense sympathy in their behaviour. Sympathy, because I had been a hardworking man and beloved to everyone before this phase of my life. If not for that love, most people would have cast me out immediately. It was almost impossible for a promising young man from a successful business family to explain to the world that he wasn't interested in making money. They never understood the satisfaction I got from helping people recover from life-threatening diseases.

It was not that I didn't know how to make money; I just wasn't interested in the worldly pleasure of money-making without a larger purpose. It was when my financial challenges became unbearable that I realised that money was necessary, too. After all, you can't fill others' cups when your own cup is empty, can you? And so, I revived myself in the business world with the help of my supporting and relentlessly encouraging wife. Today, I am a successful nutritionist who is known all over the world for his unique ability to reverse various life-threatening diseases using the right diet. And I am happy to say that I get paid handsomely for my work.

I have another business, too – it provides fire-fighting systems for commercial buildings. Both these businesses earn me enough money not only to support my needs, but also to help the less privileged.

> *I have earned back the respect and love of my family, friends and community at large. Surprisingly, today, they respect me more for my work in nutrition than for the other business I run."*

Sometimes, I wonder how society becomes insensitive and doesn't realise that just because someone is unable to follow societal norms, it doesn't mean they don't know those norms or that they are losers. It could also be because they never *wanted* to conform to the rules of society. That's why we get to see so many smart people do things they aren't 'supposed' to be doing – something different – while mediocrity is happy to take the well-trodden path. Society breeds mediocrity instead of giving birth to genuine leaders. In fact, I think it punishes leaders for thinking differently and throws additional setbacks their way. But leaders being leaders, they fight and overcome those setbacks. It's high time we realised our folly and changed the way we behave as a society.

Dr Kuiljeit Uppaal (the world's first Image Scientist, who we met in Chapter One), narrates a slightly different story. By now, you know her struggles with polio in childhood and how she overcame them subsequently. Her 'misfit story' is another compelling one. It talks about how society judges people based on their personality, choices and even actions, without taking time to understand the reality behind those choices or actions. Kuiljeit says,

> *"Confidence is something I have in abundance, and I am very comfortable in my skin because I am not in competition with anyone. I have never felt I am less than anybody else. Nor do I ever look down upon people who suffer from low confidence. I am mostly in my own space and happily so. But often, this is misinterpreted. Two incidents come to my mind as we speak.*

The first incident happened when I was newly married. I was living in a small army cantonment in a northern state of India, as my husband was in the Indian Army. He was posted at the border, and I was mostly alone in the cantonment. We had only one vehicle, and that was a Kawasaki Bajaj – my husband's motorcycle. As it was the only vehicle we had and I knew how to ride it, I would be riding it around for day-to-day commuting, doing chores, etc.

This didn't go down well with my peers, the other officers' wives. They probably didn't know how to ride or had a preconceived notion that riding bikes was a manly thing. Therefore, even without people actually knowing me, I got labelled as a snooty person. People would gossip saying, 'Oh, she is in a different league. She is a pilot, she rides a bike, she is arrogant, etc.' And I would wonder, 'If I were on a cycle, would the same social labelling happen?' Probably not. But because I was riding a motorcycle, which was supposedly a man's thing, I was being judged. Being a pilot, I was comfortable handling speed and enjoyed riding the bike at high speeds. Fortunately, cantonments have a lot of open spaces, and there is enough room for zipping around. The other women were fairly intimidated by this, and I found them keeping a distance from me until eventually, I got around to breaking the ice with them. That was when they realised how wrong they had been in judging me prematurely.

The second incident happened when a friend of mine enrolled my name for a beauty contest at the Navy Queen Ball, in which wives and daughters of defence officers participated. One of the women, who gathered that there was less participation at the ball from army wives, thought I should join the contest to improve the numbers and the chances of an army wife winning the crown. When she told me about this, I was taken aback! Taking part in a beauty contest was the last thing on my mind. However, my friend insisted and coaxed me into participating. I finally agreed for the sake of our friendship and participated.

I didn't have clothes that would supposedly suit a beauty pageant; I wore whatever I could find and participated. And even before I could realise it, I was one of the top five – the finalists! There was a 'questions and answers' round with the five finalists, and I ended up being in the top three, but I didn't win the crown. Later, I came to know from a reliable source that the judges found me 'overconfident'. It seems two of the judges commented, 'She is just too confident,' and they didn't seem to like that.

> **"I think it was the mental conditioning that a woman is supposed to be demure, subservient, slightly lower on confidence; then she comes across as more likeable. And here was this fiercely independent-thinking smart woman who was so confident and had no fears. Even when standing on stage in front of thousands of people, she didn't have an iota of under-confidence."**

That worked against me. When the source told me this, I marvelled at what mental conditioning could do to people. I believe one needs to go beyond this conditioning or at least broaden it, especially when one is sitting in a responsible position like a judge's chair.

Interestingly, instead of feeling bad about this incident, I was amused by it. 'Oh! So I lost some points because I was over-confident; how funny is that!' Very fascinatingly, when the emcee came on stage and asked the crowd to guess who would be the winner, the crowd shouted out my name and cheered for me. When the result was announced, the reality, however, was something else. For me, though, it didn't make much of a difference, as I was participating only for my friend. And my purpose of going up on that stage had anyway been fulfilled."

From Kuiljeit's story, it is clear that everyone has conscious and unconscious biases about what is 'normal'. And smart leaders not only know this, but also consciously make sure they minimise their biases (if not get rid of them completely) by being more aware of themselves and their actions.

> **PAUSE AND REFLECT**
>
> Have you been a misfit too? Or do you know someone who has been a misfit? What's your unique take on them? I'd love to hear that.
>
> Write to me at connect@srijatabhatnagar.com

I have had run-ins with society, too. As a child, I was always rebellious and different from other kids. I was outgoing, ambitious, adventurous and ready to explore the unexplored. When other kids' parents would tell them not to do something because it was dangerous, they would listen and stay put. If my parents told me not to do something, I would be sure to do it. My mother always wondered if I would fight with random people while returning from school every day. When I turned a teenager, she wouldn't be surprised if I fought with eve-teasers while coming home. No wonder, my poor parents were constantly worried about my safety and well-being!

I would race with trucks on the highway – on my tiny bicycle! One good thing was that I was a smart child who needed very little attention or effort to do well in studies. That's why I would get away with being rebellious every time. Even so, my mom's heart sank when she came to know that I wished to live alone in a new city. She was rightfully (and frightfully) worried, because she knew me well.

It had become my habit to rebel. Every time society said I shouldn't be doing this or going there or hanging around with certain people, I made sure to do that even more. When people said I shouldn't study Commerce in college ("because you are so good in studies"), I went ahead and chose Commerce. When they said that taking up a job is the way to financial independence and that doing business is risky, I said, "Bring it on, let's take some risk!" and became an entrepreneur.

They said I should marry only within my community. I promptly chose to marry someone I was compatible with, instead of worrying about which community he belonged to.

All this rebelling finally bore results. Today, the same society tells me, "Oh! You are a risk-taker and a pioneer in doing unachievable things. If you have started doing something, it will be a success." All I do is smile and let it be.

Fortunately, I have always found my parents, spouse and daughter beside me every time I took a risk. Every time I wanted to attempt something new, they have cheered for me.

So much so, that this book wouldn't have been possible without their support – especially that of my daughter, who kept asking me about its progress.

> **My learning has been that it's good to be rebellious, as long as you stick to your convictions and go after a strong purpose. It's good to honour your uniqueness. That's your identity. But don't be rebellious for the sake of being rebellious.**

Learnings

Today, I tell people to embrace their unique quality of being a misfit. Because only misfits:

- can teach everyone the lesson that even if no one comes to your rescue, you'd better buck up and fight for yourself;
- can be content with helping others, instead of playing a mindless money-making game;
- can ask questions about their purpose, and have the courage and willingness to change the world;
- know that it's the conscious and unconscious biases of people that encourage them to judge others;
- can laugh at those who expect them to behave in a certain way, because that's the 'norm'.

When he was a child, one of my male coaching clients was termed as 'weak' and 'too feminine'; because of this labelling, he still suffers from an identity crisis. After beginning to work with me, he is slowly exploring his identity more openly.

Life lesson: ***Only when you are authentic with yourself, can you be authentic with others. Therefore, be your most authentic 'misfit' self.***

Also, to the world, I would like to say: instead of judging others for their uniqueness, look at them with compassion. Judging others can not only be erroneous, but can also expose your rigid and unlikeable face. People who are quick to judge others and form an opinion are the biggest losers in the world. They lose an opportunity to expand their worldview. Also, they miss the chance to make exciting connections. They behave like a frog in the well, which thinks that the well is the entire universe!

But how to stop the temptation to judge and label people? Every time you find yourself judging someone, especially when you don't know them well enough, do the following:

> **PAUSE AND REFLECT**
>
> - Remember that one can never know all the aspects of someone's life and personality.
>
> - Ask yourself if you know that person well – personally, professionally, spiritually and emotionally.
>
> - A 360-degree view is a myth. You can never have a 360-degree view of something, unless you are rotating. Are you turning yourself around?
>
> - Replace criticism with compassion, and you will see that you form a better opinion about others.

✦✦✦

Have you ever failed in entrepreneurship or lost a lot of money in business? Have you ever wanted to be an entrepreneur? Do you think it is cool to start a venture? A popular perception is that start-up founders are lucky, because they can choose when to work and when not to, they can do what they want to and they make a lot of money. The fact, however, is that the start-up journey is full of twists and turns, ups and downs. It has several unimaginable, unpredictable hurdles.

In the next chapter, we will talk about another biggie – setbacks related to entrepreneurship and start-ups. Our leaders' stories will give you a peek into their professional lives and how they tackled their setbacks. Are you ready for them?

CHAPTER 5

Venture Misadventure

BRANDI BENSON

I asked **Brandi Benson** (https://brandilbenson.com/) if she had failed in entrepreneurship or had lost money in business. The question resonated very well with her.

Brandi is an entrepreneur, writer, speaker and cancer survivor from the United States of America. She is the founder and CEO of Resume-Advantage, an employment service for civilians and transitioning military veterans. She is a former US Army veteran who was deployed in Iraq in 2009. Her debut book *'The Enemy Inside Me'* tells the touching story of her Ewing Sarcoma cancer diagnosis during her deployment in Iraq as a soldier. She is currently pursuing a PhD in Education from Concordia University in Chicago. She gives us her take on the issue of business setbacks and how to face them:

> *I feel like it's been around forever. I wouldn't call these setbacks because they are more like learning experiences for me – being an entrepreneur and burning from the bottom, coming up and learning how to do things right, who to talk to or finding the blueprint for success. But you know what, there **is** no blueprint for success; that's a myth. Every company, every organisation, every client, every entrepreneur, every situation is different. Therefore, the blueprint for their success is also different. When people tell you, 'This is how I did it, this is how you need to do it', that may or may not work for another person.*
>
> *I went with the flow, learning by making mistakes. All I knew was I wanted my clients to have excellent customer service and a great experience working with us. How did I do that and how am I still doing it? I lend myself out there. Being a polite person and having excellent listening skills helps. I have learnt from each of my experiences. I am having a lot of setbacks, like financial or workforce-related issues, but I also know that these life lessons are inevitable for my business growth and success.*
>
> *To people who are going through a professional setback right now, I would like to say, 'Avoid making a permanent decision based on a temporary situation. You may have lost a big client, lost money in business or had to shut down a business. These are all temporary things. Just because of speed-breakers, don't stop the journey towards your destination. Never give up on your dreams or forget your true self. We have so much time to live; we don't need to give up everything because of these temporary hiccups.'*
>
> *Know that one wrong decision can take many years to fix, and you don't want to do that. All you need to do is go with the*

flow and keep an eye on the big picture at the same time. When you see doors closing in front of you, remember that there are many other doors open. All you need to do is to turn yourself towards the open doors."

How often do we see people showing the maturity to accept setbacks as learning experiences? Even I couldn't do that when I failed to make EthnicShack, my first start-up, a successful one. Eventually, I did learn from that setback; just that it was an expensive lesson!

I remember a specific experience that changed my perspective towards business setbacks forever. My business partner and I were going to meet a client. It was an important client, and we were upbeat that we will crack the business. At the same time, we were nervous, too.

When we were about to enter the client's office, I tried pushing the door. But the door wouldn't open. I kept pushing it, but it remained shut. After a few minutes of continuous pushing and the door not opening, I was about to give up. At that moment, my partner said, "Why not try pulling the door, instead?" And guess what? The door opened smoothly when I pulled it!

Come to think of it, most often, we are either pushing when we need to pull or are merely knocking on a closed-door, failing to see there is an open door just around the corner.

In the previous chapter, we read about how **Nikhil Chaudhary** became the subject of society's ridicule and judgement because of his multiple business setbacks. Now let's understand what exactly went wrong with his businesses. Coming from a successful business family, it was apparent that he had always dreamt of becoming an entrepreneur. But, even after knowing the rules of the game well and getting trained from childhood to be an entrepreneur, Nikhil had his share of problems along the way. He explains,

"Right from childhood, I wanted to be an entrepreneur. My journey of becoming one began after my graduation. Within a few months of starting my business, it was flourishing so well that I needed more support to manage it better. My dad eventually joined me, and we quickly became the top dealer for a mobile phone brand. But suddenly, the brand decided to close down as they were suffering huge losses and that's when my business also experienced a considerable loss.

As people say, 'quick to rise, quicker to set'. Something similar happened to me, too – from a dream run in the business to no work and a pile of debt within a few months. Even worse, my dad's health deteriorated sharply due to this debacle. Seeing the mental turmoil caused by the loss of business and money, and dad's deteriorating health, my maternal grandmother offered to take dad with her, so that they could help him recover his health and I could focus on work.

During this period, I experimented with many business ideas. I started a venture in car accessories, with no prior experience in that line of business. I started it because my neighbour was very successful in the field, and I assumed I could make it big, too. It failed. Stupid, wasn't I? No wonder it tanked. And soon, I was left with an empty shop which I was about to close. Instead, I ended up opening a chaat and Indian snacks outlet called 'Chennai Chaupati'. It served tea, samosa, panipuri and other fast food to customers. I started this in partnership with someone who saw great potential in me and who was ready to invest money in the outlet. Unfortunately, this venture failed, too. Later, I realised I was partnering with the wrong kind of people. They were all good people, but they lacked the right business knowledge.

Knowing every rule of the business and still being unable to make it big in my game was getting onto my nerves. On top of that, there was the stress of my dad being unwell. It felt like a *double whammy. I was losing interest in business and beginning to lean towards social work. It was only after a lot of motivational counselling from my wife and encouraging friends that I returned to the business world – after seven long years!*

Now, I ensure that I collaborate only with the right people while doing business. Today, I am a successful nutritionist and run another very successful company simultaneously. That company is a partnership venture too, but the credit for its success goes more to my partner than to me. Initially, I used to be very uncomfortable with him. But I knew he was the right person, who had done the right things to be successful.

My business partner moulded me and brought the best out of me. He taught me that one should deal only with decision-makers while doing business. My company is among the top three vendors in the field of fire-fighting material in the states of Telangana and Andhra Pradesh in India. It is in its third year now, with a turnover of over Indian Rupees (INR) 100 million.

This attitude of collaborating with the right people also helped me grow my nutrition counselling as a business and to work with people who can truly bring about change in the world. From being a flop and the owner of a fast food joint to becoming a world-renowned nutritionist and a successful entrepreneur – it has been a long journey, indeed!

Every step of this journey was chiselled with pain. But I never compromised on my values. I never cheated anyone to make money. Even in the businesses that failed, my associates never faced losses. Even today, they are ready to work with me. On the other hand, the support of my friends, family and well-wishers always ensured my success.

My failures taught me some valuable lessons in life. Today, when I see many entrepreneurs ready to change the world with their raw business ideas, I tell them to go slow and steady.

> "If you aim for the stars and jump from your terrace, most likely you will fall flat on your face. Sometimes the fall can be so bad that getting up again may become difficult. It's better to keep building on your terrace and someday, you will get closer to the stars."

I believe three things put people on the priority list of failures: indecisiveness, taking quick decisions without clear thinking and decision-making based on others' opinions alone. Avoiding these are my big secrets to success. Watch out for these three if you want to be successful in life."

Just because one knows all the rules of the game, one cannot win every single time. Sometimes, external factors create an adverse situation where one has very little control.

It's essential to realise that even seasoned professionals have to enhance their skills and get mentored to keep improving their game. Like Nikhil did.

Are you ready to do so, too?

Dr Kuiljeit Uppaal (the renowned polymath we met in Chapter 1) had to face another kind of entrepreneurial setback. She worked in the corporate world for a long time and then moved on to start her business. Let's hear about her experience in her own words:

> *"When I turned into an entrepreneur, my very first client took all the work from me and never paid up. I had worked hard on the project for six months and made sure that I had given the best results, exactly the way my client had wanted. And yet, she did not pay me. It was a rude shock for me! That was the first time I had to come to terms with the harsh reality of people cheating you.*
>
> *She was a significantly influential client, and I didn't have the financial capability to get into a legal battle with her. I was disappointed, but in my mind, I told myself that maybe the money was never meant to be mine. This was probably supposed to be only a learning experience for me with regard to how people can*

be and how an entrepreneur always needs to have her system in place from the beginning. When you are an employee, the story is very different. But the moment you turn into an entrepreneur, the things you get exposed to are of a different nature altogether. Despite having a contract with her and my full faith in her, my client still ditched me when it came to the fees. Till that point, I never knew why companies took payment advances; after this incident, I learnt why. I discovered it the hard way, but in one sense, I am happy it happened.

Since then, I have started taking an advance from clients on payments. And today, most of my payments come on time. I would be foolish if I didn't learn from that setback and continued the same way as I did earlier, even after losing lakhs of rupees. Sometimes, it becomes costly to learn a lesson or two. But it is always worth it."

What happened to Kuiljeit happens to a lot of other entrepreneurs, too. They learn the tricks of the business the hard way. The excitement of starting up is so high, that first-time entrepreneurs miss out on the more delicate yet important points.

> **PAUSE AND REFLECT**
>
> Are you an entrepreneur? Are you able to relate to the setbacks mentioned in this chapter? How did you tackle *your* setbacks?
>
> Do our leaders' stories help you? Will you change the way you deal with your start-up/business challenges after reading their stories?
>
> Do you need any advice on how to turn your start-up setback into a success? Feel free to email me at connect@srijatabhatnagar.com

In my life as an entrepreneur, I have missed the more delicate points, too but eventually, learnt my lessons. It was costly, yet it made a lot of difference.

As you saw in Chapter Two, I had a bad experience with my new boss at work and because of that, had to suffer a demotion too. Of course, the victim mentality kicked in, initially; I participated in a blame game. Finally, however, I decided to move on. To a better career, better place, better boss and better everything. Don't we all look for better things in life, always?

I found a better life, but only temporarily. I was always terrified of losing my job, and I did lose my job! The start-up I moved to closed down within 11 months of its inception. That too, at a most unexpected time, slapping a forced sabbatical upon me.

I was mad, depressed, upset and angry. Above all, I started doubting my capabilities. In my mind, I became a victim once again. This went for a month or so. During this time, I kept browsing the internet for random things. And that's how I chanced upon the concept of "victim mindset vs survivor mindset".

This spurred a change in my attitude. I decided to utilise my sabbatical for better things. I had gained a lot of weight after my pregnancy, thanks to the sudden surge in my stress level. Choosing to concentrate on my health, I started working out. Initially, I would take out all my pent-up anger on the machines during my workouts. Eventually, I started noticing a change in my mood. I was feeling happier, lighter and active. I lost 8 kgs (17.6 lbs) in 3 months – my highest weight loss in three months. I travelled to meet long-lost friends and family, which brightened my mood further.

> This sense of re-bonding and connection helped me regain my confidence. Slowly, I started becoming calm outside and fierce inside. I started thinking of self-employment as a way to live a life of my own. I rekindled my dream – the dream of becoming an entrepreneur.

I started researching different problems/needs in the market, based on which I could possibly build a start-up. I still have the list of more than 500 start-up ideas that I wrote down back then. It took almost two years of research and deliberation to zero down on my final plan.

The moment I finalised my business idea, I was over the moon! As if the start-up had already succeeded. I bet a lot of entrepreneurs think the same way. Little did I know that this was just the beginning.

Thanks to the excitement and over-enthusiasm, we went ahead and spent a lot of money on things that didn't matter much to our venture. Let me be honest – we splurged. Instead of concentrating on the product-market fit and revenues, we focused on a good looking office, fancy videos, a pitch deck that looked amazing, etc. That turned out to be disastrous. Within eighteen months of starting up, we were struggling to make both ends meet. We poured in a lot of capital, but nothing seemed to work. Around the same time, I was fortunate enough to get a chance to study 'Entrepreneurship Management' at the prestigious Indian Institute of Management (IIM), Bangalore. I thought, "Wow! I am not only getting a chance to live my dream of studying at an IIM, but also a chance to revive my start-up."

After sitting through the classes and mentoring sessions at IIM, I realised that EthnicShack (my company) had a dead business model. There was not much life left in it. The best option was to shut it down. And that's exactly what I did, though with a very heavy heart. It was almost like killing my child!

As I was recuperating from the pain of shutting EthnicShack, the idea of Ridhani was planted in my head. The corridor conversations I had with my IIM Bangalore batchmates helped me realise how underserved the women's professional wear segment was in India. Working women here never found the balanced combination of comfort, design and uniqueness in their professional outfits. I did extensive research this time to validate my hypothesis and finally, Ridhani was born – for women professionals by women professionals. I feel proud to say that today, the brand has captured the hearts of its customers with its custom-made work wear for women, personalised customer service and attention to detail.

Learnings

Some of the priceless learnings from the start-up setbacks and responses we read about in this chapter are:

- Become an entrepreneur only if you think it is your calling; not because your friends or neighbours are entrepreneurs.
- Get into a business only if *you* are comfortable with it and not because someone else is successful in it.
- When you treat setbacks as learning experiences, the journey becomes more manageable and fruitful.
- When pushing a door does not open it, try pulling it. Also, instead of banging on a closed door, concentrate on open doors for better results.
- Just because you are a pro at something, it doesn't mean that you will never fail. Sometimes, setbacks are also a result of external variables that are not under your control.
- Entrepreneurship comes with various pitfalls. One of them is not having proper systems and processes. So make sure you have those in place right from the beginning. Along with that, well-defined objectives, key results areas, clear policies and controls are also needed to achieve the desired outcome.
- In any business, focus on the basics – that's revenue and profit-generation. Once that's sorted, everything else will fall in place.

It took me time to recognise the lessons from my experiences. I was too deep in the victim zone. Like others who have fallen into this trap, I cribbed at my fate, wondered 'why me', blamed things like people's enmity against me, my bad luck and wrong timing. Most damagingly, I began thinking that I wasn't capable enough!

Fortunately, I learnt my lessons eventually. And the most important of them all was that things often happen to you, not because of your mistake or because others are being mean to you. Things happen because that's the best way for you to learn valuable lessons. I was refusing to learn my lessons. Hence the Universe threw me into a zone where I had to be more vulnerable to accept, acknowledge and learn. Like the famous saying goes, "What doesn't kill you makes you stronger." I survived the blow and became wiser, stronger and smarter.

Surrendering to the Universe and its ways is most important in times of hardship. When you learn this art, you become more aware of your surroundings and the riches you are gifted with. When you surrender, you get more attuned to possible solutions – because you stop resisting and start looking for a way out of your shitty comfort zone.

> **PAUSE AND REFLECT**
>
> My advice to budding as well as struggling entrepreneurs, is:
>
> - Evaluate yourself first before plunging into entrepreneurship. Ask yourself if it is meant for you.
> - Ask yourself if you are ready for everything that comes along with entrepreneurship – the good, the bad and the ugly.
> - Please be very careful about where you invest or spend your money, if and after you have decided to start your own venture.
> - Ask yourself this question – "Is this business going to earn me money?" Move forward only if the answer is a resounding YES.

Life lesson: *Every setback in life comes to prepare us for future challenges, making us a better version of ourselves.*

We always look at setbacks as problems and resist change. When we surrender and stop resisting the changes, we are in a better position to pick up the opportunities that life gives us.

It took me two years to spot those opportunities, because I was unsure of unknown pastures and hence, scared to take a step towards a strange journey.

But eventually, when I did take that step, I couldn't have been happier! My mindset changed forever. Today, I jump at the unknown and fearlessly attempt anything new. Instead of asking, *"How will I do it?"* I now ask, *"Why do I want to do it? Why not try it? What will it take for me to do it?"*

✦ ✦ ✦

In the next chapter, we will dive deep into financial setbacks and how they can ruin not only an individual but also an entire family. Are you going through a financial challenge at present? Or, have you been through one before?

Most leaders have been through financial setbacks in life. Some, of course, were born rich, but circumstances took them through challenging times. Others have seen difficult times as a child, due to their humble beginnings. The similarity between both types of leaders, though, is that they all rose up from their limitations and created abundance in more than one way.

Each experience is fascinating. Come, let's read about them.

CHAPTER 6

Capital Mistakes

Financial setbacks are common – either early in life or due to particular circumstances later on. Unfortunately, while we learn several other things in school, we don't get to learn how to manage our finances. Nor do the majority of us get to learn this from our family. It is strange that in India, money is believed to be Godly, but those having a lot of money are often seen as people with low morals – greedy or corrupt. Beliefs such as "business people are a corrupted bunch" and "you should earn money, but not so much that you lose your humility" are imparted to us from childhood.

Fortunately for **Nikhil Chaudhary** (who we first met in Chapter Four), he learnt the techniques of managing money well from childhood, thanks to his family's business background. Being raised in one of the most influential business families in Nepal made a big difference to him. In his own words:

> *"I was born with a golden spoon in my mouth. As a young boy, I had seen every possible luxury of life. In those days, when even travelling by autorickshaw was a luxury in Nepal, we owned cars. We used to take holidays every year. My dad had around 200 employees. I studied in one of the most expensive boarding schools in India. God blessed me with so much opulence early in my life, that I never feel jealous of anyone else's achievements and wealth.*
>
> *But, there came a time in my life when some people my dad had trusted ran away with a lot of his hard-earned money. I was in India at that time. I told him I would set up a business here. After setting up a mobile phone dealership, I requested him to*

join me in managing the same, as the company was growing by leaps and bounds. The demand for mobile phones was picking up in India, and everyone wanted a mobile phone. I built the market quickly and we became one of the highest-selling dealerships in all of India. Unfortunately, the phone brand incurred losses and had to shut down the business. It came as a sudden and rude shock to me and my dealership. In the process, I lost a lot of money, too.

That was a severe financial struggle I have faced in my life, but because of my attitude, the struggle continued for much longer than it should have. My attitude towards money had changed to, 'Why should I earn money when my loved ones are not happy? What's the point in all this?'

When I was a child, I used to spend a lot of time with my grandfather. He would always say, 'If you want to make someone feel miserable, all you have to do is to give them all the luxuries of life for a few days and then bring them back to where they came from. They will feel miserable about the luxury they experienced for some time, but which they don't have now.' This thought had remained with me. After enjoying all the luxuries of life, I went to the space I originally started from. And thinking again and again of the wrong decisions that had made me lose money kept me in my miserable state for a long time.

It was a long learning stint for me. Finally, our financial problem spiralled up unbearably. It was a long heart-to-heart conversation with my wife that made me realise that my thought process and decisions were all wrong. I realised that she deserved a better life. That's how I sprung back. And within two years, I not only recovered all that I had lost monetarily, but also earned much more than I ever had earlier.

The financial problems in my life were an outcome of my choices and the financial freedom I enjoy today is also an outcome of my choices. In sum, it is the attitude that matters! The money follows, inwards or outwards."

Many youngsters take decisions that aren't productive or empowering to start with, as Nikhil did in the initial years of his adult life. Like any other setback, financial setbacks can occur for various reasons. Sometimes, it is because of a situation, sometimes it is because of lacking financial literacy and sometimes, it is merely due to bad luck. But the worst thing you can do when faced with such a setback is to decide to remain in that struggle. To get hit by a financial setback is circumstantial, but to decide to stay in that or to move on is a choice – *your choice.*

What choice do you want to make?

Sagar Amlani faced a different kind of financial setback. Though he was born in a lower-middle-class family, he and his family knew how to run the house within their budget constraints. But just when life had become slightly more comfortable, their financial setback came along. Sagar recalls that phase clearly:

"This incident occurred when I was in the UK, doing my post-graduation and working.

Those days, my father's earnings were about INR 3000-3500 per month, a small sum of money. My mother's tuitions used to earn her around INR 6000-7000 per month. Our total household earning was, therefore, around INR 10,000 per month. My brother was studying Engineering. They were still living in a chawl. Our financial condition was already stressful. In that situation, when I got a chance to go to the UK, that too on a scholarship, I grabbed it immediately. I wanted to quickly complete my post-graduation and earn so much that my family could buy a decent apartment and move out of the chawl at the earliest.

In the UK, I used to take tuitions to supplement my income. I would send whatever I earned to my dad back in Mumbai, so that my family could save up to buy a house. Every time I would send money, he would visit the same money exchange bureau to exchange currencies and withdraw the money. The first three times, he smoothly got the British Pounds converted to Indian Rupees. The fourth time, he went to exchange 1200 Pounds. After withdrawing the money, he was returning with around INR 1,00,000, when he was waylaid by four people. All of them were well-built and over 6 feet in height. They claimed to be from the Income Tax department and accused dad of carrying black money. Dad responded, saying, 'No, this is not black money!' Then they asked him, 'Why are you coming out of that money exchange bureau? They have been caught for laundering black money and now you will be caught, too!'

My dad was shit scared! He wondered what was going on and what he should do. One of the men said authoritatively that unless my dad showed them what he had in his bag, they would take him to the CBI (Central Bureau of Investigation). Dad told the men he was carrying his son's hard-earned money. 'We are very poor. My son is in the UK. He works there and sends us some money', he said. The men rubbished his story and said they would take him with them, get my visa cancelled and make sure I go to prison in the UK. Dad was so scared by their threats, that he pleaded with them to take some of the money from whatever he had and let him go. But those people insisted that he would be allowed to go only if he handed over the entire money to them.

Finally, dad gave them all the money he had and left.

He went away somewhere and switched off his phone. When he didn't return for 3 hours, mom called me and told me that he had gone to collect the cash, but hadn't returned home yet. I knew the bureau where dad would go to collect the money. And so, I called them. They told me someone had robbed dad and gave me all the finer details of what had happened to him. I felt someone could give details of that kind only if they were involved in the incident themselves. I realised that it had been a trap set up by the money exchanger and those four guys, because they knew my dad would come to collect the money that day. They robbed him by emotionally blackmailing him. Though I knew those people were the culprits, I couldn't do much from the UK.

My priority was to find dad and see if he was alright. For a person who earned a mere INR 3500 per month, losing INR 1,00,000 was surely a big blow! And so, all of us were worried about his well-being. Finally, after three hours, he came home, depressed. When I called him, he started crying. I calmed him down and asked him what exactly had happened. When he said he had lost INR 1,00,000, I went into shock immediately, because that was a significant amount for me, too! In that shock, I wasn't in a position to listen to anything else. I just told dad it was alright and that I would earn more to make up for that loss. After this, I slid into self-pity. I started blaming myself and wondered how I was going to recover all that money.

My maternal aunt, with whom I was living in London, saw me lost and dejected. She spoke to my mom and came to know of the whole story. That's when she sat with me and said, 'Why are you crying over what is lost? Can you recover it?' I was in no mood to listen to her preaching and yelled at her. She yelled back at me saying, 'Why can't you earn that money back? In fact, why can't you earn more than that? Why can't you put in more effort and work overtime?'

That's when her key message hit me. I started working harder. Taking up a litter picker's job, I started waking up at 4 am. The job paid me well, and within 20 days, I had earned 1400 Pounds. This was an extra income that wouldn't have come my way if we hadn't lost that money back in India. I continued with that job because I wanted to earn much more than 1400 pounds. And that's how I bounced back. Within a month, I sent dad double the money. I thanked him for having lost the money earlier, for only because of that could I create an opportunity to earn more."

It's so important to be careful about finances, especially monetary transactions. What happened to Sagar and his family can happen to any one of us, because we are never taught the precautions we need to take while handling money.

> As children, we are never taught the difference between working for money vs making money work for us. We are never taught the difference between the need for money vs the want for money. We aren't taught how to make our money grow or the difference between investments and expenses. As a result, most of us grow up having distorted views and beliefs about money.

PAUSE AND REFLECT

Have you experienced a financial setback? Have you been through it or are you going through it now?

How did you deal with it? Will your approach change, now that you have read Nikhil's and Sagar's stories?

If you need help in getting past your financial setbacks, write to me without inhibition at connect@srijatabhatnagar.com

I had distorted views and beliefs about money, too. When I was working in the corporate world, I used to earn a handsome salary every month. I used to spend the bulk of it on buying the latest smartphone, other gadgets, trendy clothes, shoes or junk jewellery. Sometimes, I'd use my credit cards and convert the spends into EMIs. Eventually, my habit of instant gratification and delayed payment meant that I had to pay a huge amount as interest to the credit card companies.

When I moved to entrepreneurship from being an employee, I put the bulk of my savings into my start-up. However, many items that I thought were investments actually turned out to be expenses! I never knew the real difference between investment and expenditure. That worsened the problem. Because I didn't know the correct way of managing money, I lost INR 2.5 million in business. This setback broke my back so severely, that it took me six long years to recover from it!

I had to go through immense mental agony to unlearn my old unproductive habits and cultivate productive money-management habits. I not only attended multiple seminars and workshops to learn better financial management, but also read the book 'Rich Dad Poor Dad' by Robert Kiyosaki. This has been one of the best books I have read about money management. It not only changed my thought process, but also helped me learn more productive techniques to manage my personal finance. When I finally understood the difference between investment and expense in the real sense, I started improving my situation.

Today, I am a careful spender. I spend only on things that I need; I indulge very rarely. My spending and saving patterns have drastically changed. This helps me manage my finance so well, that I have stopped feeling constrained for money.

Learnings

Some of the crucial points you can learn from Nikhil's, Sagar's and my financial setbacks are:

- ✦ Have a balanced attitude towards managing personal finance. Ask yourself if your attitude is helping your loved ones and yourself.
- ✦ Beware of taking unproductive decisions around money. Even if you take a wrong decision by mistake, know that you can come out of it, provided you *want* to come out of it.
- ✦ Protect your money like a hawk; never carry out monetary transactions sloppily.
- ✦ There is no shame in learning and enhancing your financial knowledge, even if it is later in life. It is never too late. I recommend that you read the book 'Rich Dad Poor Dad' for

some powerful lessons on handling money. Also, attending good workshops or seminars on personal finance could help you a lot.
- It is essential to know the difference between investment and expenses. Take every opportunity you can to see the difference between them. To be sure, take the advice of a good, qualified financial advisor.
- When faced with a setback, you may have to work doubly hard to overcome it and recover your money. Remember, working smart is as important as working hard.

If you are going through financial challenges at present, I invite you to take a close look at your income and expenditure.

> **PAUSE AND REFLECT**
>
> - Every day for 30 days, note down every expense you incur. Write down even the smallest of expenses – whether you are spending money on food, travel, utility bills, credit card bills, etc.
> - After that, mark out the most significant expenses on that list.
> - Ask yourself if each one of these expenses is a necessity. Can you survive without any of them? Be brutally honest with yourself. If you really cannot do with an expense item, it is a 'need'. Everything else is a 'want'.
> - Once you separate your 'wants' from your 'needs', all you have to do is reduce the amount you spend on 'wants'.
>
> Within three months, your financial condition will improve.
>
> Go ahead, attempt it and feel free to let me know how your situation changed. Write to me at connect@srijatabhatnagar.com

Life lesson: *You always have enough money for your needs, but not for your wants. Keep track of your needs to keep your finances healthy.*

✦✦✦

In the next chapter, we will talk about another human-made setback. Have you been betrayed by anybody? Have you been taken for granted by someone or has someone backstabbed you? If yes, how did you respond to that situation?

May I encourage you to write down your answers on a sheet of paper before moving to the next chapter?

CHAPTER 7

A Single Stab, A Hundred Wounds

Many of my clients say that they find it difficult to trust people because someone has backstabbed them in the past. Or, that they have been taken for granted by someone or the other, because of which they don't trust anyone easily today.

I thought, "Why not put this question to a few leaders and see what they have to say about it?" And when I did so, some surprising insights came tumbling out!

Often, when I coach people on turning setbacks into successes, I hear them say that one of the biggest challenges they face is a betrayal. Some of them say their friends betrayed them. And so, they have lost faith in friendship. Some others say their co-workers backstabbed them for a coveted promotion. Consequently, they have stopped trusting their co-workers. Some say their partners lied to them and had extramarital affairs, because of which they have lost faith in love. There are many other such cases of betrayal.

I have had my share of betrayals too, about which I will tell you a little later. What about our leaders – have they ever been betrayed? How did they deal with it? As a result of being betrayed, did they change their core self, or did they remain the same person? What happened when their closed ones left them in the middle of a crisis?

We learnt about **Brandi Benson**'s start-up setback in Chapter Five. However, about a decade ago, she suffered another blow, when someone close to her betrayed her. That too, in the midst of the most significant challenge of her life – when she was already suffering from cancer! Let's hear the turn of events from Brandi herself:

> "I got married really young. My husband used to play basketball then and would go out of station for his games, tournaments, etc. Or at least, that's what he told me. Sometimes, he would return with money; sometimes, he would come back without pay. Eventually, I figured out that he wasn't travelling for basketball at all; he was going to meet a woman he had been dating for more than nine months, right under my nose. And I hadn't even known it! I discovered this accidentally one day, during the time I was down with cancer. One day, when I checked his phone for some reason, I found some objectionable text messages from another woman. I found a voice mail from her, too, in which she talked about how much she loved him and how she was looking forward to starting a family with him in Los Angeles.
>
> Already, I was having physical, mental and emotional problems because of the cancer treatment. I remember thinking that my partner should have been around me, supporting me as I was swinging between life and death. Instead, he was finding a thousand excuses for not being around!
>
> In fact, he was lying to me that he needed to shift to Los Angeles because he had received a modelling contract. I was so naïve, that without realising what was going on, I told him, 'That's alright. Whatever you need to do to get your career in shape, go ahead and do it. We remain married and will support each other's needs.' I was playing the good wife to him, though I was unwell. And this man was preparing to abandon me forever to be with another woman, that too sneakily.
>
> In the US, they say that if you get married before the age of 25, the divorce rate is likely to be 75%. I didn't believe in those statistics then. Now I know that the data was not lying. My husband fell out of love with me because I was sick with cancer, and he couldn't handle it; it was too much for him.

I ended up talking to the other woman and confronting her. She accepted all of what was going on – how long they had been dating, what their plans were and so on. It turned out that my husband had lied to her, too! He had lied about our relationship, about his name, where he lived and what his occupation was. He had pretended to be a big celebrity. As a result of my chat with that woman, her relationship with my husband fell through.

"My husband and I got divorced. I was devastated and cried a lot. It hurt me to the core. But, I had to tell myself that I deserved far better. I was worth way more than this. I needed to value myself. If I stayed with him, I would be encouraging his atrocious behaviour. And I couldn't do that."

If I continued staying with him, I'd be signalling to him that I didn't matter and that he could step over me and treat me like a piece of dirt. I had a young nephew, and I didn't want him to learn a wrong lesson. And so, I had to muster up the courage to let my husband go. He wasn't the right man for me. He was not only unavailable for me when I needed him the most, but was also happily leaving me for another woman in the middle of the most significant setback of my life (about which we will read more in Chapter Nine).

If a marriage doesn't have love and mutual respect, it is not a marriage at all. It's a compromise, and life can't be run on compromises. If your partner is betraying you, he or she isn't invested in you; there is no point in that relationship at all."

So true! If a relationship doesn't have mutual respect and love, what's the point in continuing with it? We see a number of respectless and loveless marriages, in which either partner pretends to be invested in the marriage when they are not. Often, one partner betrays the other by having an extramarital affair. Ironically though, if the other partner did the same thing to them, they wouldn't be able to tolerate it!

I'd just tell these people, who are spending their lives rowing in two boats, to stop wasting their energy on unfruitful things only because they can't muster up the courage to row steadily in one boat. And to people who tolerate and condone their partner's betrayal, I would say, "You are worth way more than this. You don't need to kill your heart and your self-respect for your heartless partner."

In the last couple of chapters, we read about the various setbacks **Nikhil Chaudhary** had to go through. Nikhil's take on betrayals is unique. He is one of the most helpful and soft-spoken people I know and is a real giver. Generally, people do take him for granted thinking that just because his style isn't aggressive, he is not a leader. Nikhil says,

> "I have let a lot of people take advantage of me several times. Not that I didn't know they were taking advantage of me. Inspite of knowing that, I let them do so. Even today, I have the same approach.
>
> It is a conscious decision, because I feel that if people can take something out of me, let them. It only means that I have something they need or want. It's my helping attitude that allows me to behave in this manner. The problem is that sometimes, people think, 'This guy gets fooled easily; so let me fool him and take whatever I can.'
>
> On the contrary, I see them as being needy. I'd like to help them until it starts hurting me. The moment it starts bothering me, I immediately stop it, confront them, and if required, cut them out from my life.
>
> Because of my wealthy background and the privilege of having seen everything in abundance as a child, I have never developed the habit of holding back while helping anyone. My dad would always say, 'When people need help, go ahead and help them without expecting anything in return.' Because, when you don't expect any return, you don't have that pinching feeling of betrayal. Plus, when people take undue advantage, they will be unable to come back to you for more help. In either case, it's a win for you.'

> *Giving without any expectation is the quality of strong leaders. Just think that God has made you capable enough to be of help to someone. And if someone helps you in return, it's always a bonus."*

Even though Nikhil is not talking about a particular setback here, I found his approach to the subject of betrayal and expectations fascinating.

"How many of us understand the concept of giving freely without any expectation in return? Also, how many of us have the maturity to realise that giving doesn't mean hurting yourself? Having an open mind and heart is essential when working with people. This helps you keep your expectation to a minimum."

When you have no expectation, you won't be disappointed or feel betrayed. And, you always have the choice to stop yourself when your 'giving' starts hurting you.

> **PAUSE AND REFLECT**
>
> Have you ever felt betrayed by someone else? How did you deal with it?
>
> After reading Brandi's and Nikhil's experiences, do you think your approach will change?
>
> Feel free to email me at connect@srijatabhatnagar.com to share your thoughts.

When Nikhil told me his story, an incident from my life came rushing to my mind.

I had a partner in my business. I took care of customer acquisitions, marketing and sales, while my partner's responsibility was the execution and timely delivery of orders.

When my father was undergoing treatment for cancer, I couldn't concentrate on the day-to-day business operations properly for almost 3 or 4 months, as I was one of his primary caregivers. At that time, we received a prestigious order. Before going ahead and committing to the customer, I checked with my business partner if we had the bandwidth and skillsets to execute that order. I sought her full involvement and cooperation in completing the order, and told her that I might not be able to focus on the fieldwork and execution, as I needed to stay by my father's side. She agreed enthusiastically and assured me that she would lead this project from the front. I managed the initial specifications-gathering, expectation-setting, budgeting, etc. and passed the baton on to her.

My partner kept assuring me that the order would be ready well before time. Generally, we would keep a buffer of 2-3 weeks in committing the date of delivery to customers. In this case, we had a whole month to execute the order. I couldn't go to the production house to check the progress. Every time I called my partner, she would say that things were progressing well. Usually, our internal delivery date would be 3 or 4 days before the delivery date committed to the customer – to help us tackle any unforeseen delay. On the internal delivery date, my partner said that there were some unexpected delays, but that the order would be delivered on the date committed to the customer. Imagine my shock when, a day before the customer delivery date, she told me that the people who were executing the project had disappeared with the raw materials!

I lost my patience then. I knew there was no point in asking her to sort out the issue. And so, leaving my ailing father with my mother and husband, I decided to sort the problem out myself. Obviously, we couldn't deliver what the customer had asked for, but I managed the situation somehow, by giving her something that would meet her need to some extent.

Failing to deliver this order, our business reputation suffered a big blow. Also, this incident showed me my business partner's true capabilities and credibility (or rather, the lack of them). I slowed down our work for the time being. I had to concentrate on my father's health and clear the mess that had been created in our business. Just as I was mulling having an open conversation with my partner and allowing her to explain her side of the story, she resigned from her post with immediate effect by just sending me a WhatsApp message! I accepted her resignation without any fuss and told her to send me a formal resignation over email. All these years later, I am yet to receive that email.

Three months after that incident, I discovered the same products that had 'gone missing'. And I came to know a very different version of the story. This version not only sounded mysterious, but also pointed a finger at my business partner for the fiasco.

This incident made me realise that we don't always know the truth. Some people do things for reasons known only to them. Fretting over these incidents would be stupid. And so, instead of digging deeper into the issue, I chose to leave it right there. I had learnt a valuable lesson on trust and credibility. I picked up the products and belatedly delivered them to the customer.

> **Today, I still trust people with an open heart, but take them through random 'checkpoints' before giving them any important task. This helps me assess the level of confidence I can have on them. Also, I work only with people who have a high level of integrity and credibility.**

At the same time, I don't evaluate or judge a person based on someone else's performance. I work on a clean slate with everybody and my opinion about someone is only about them; I don't extrapolate it to anybody else.

Learnings

As usual, we can mine a few golden nuggets from these stories:

- ✦ In any relationship, trust has to be mutual. Establishing that trust with you is the responsibility of the other person.

- Your responsibility is to have an open mind and give the other person multiple chances to establish trust. But if and when they fail to do so, you should never feel bad about it.
- Stop wasting your energy and time with disrespectful and irresponsible partners, be it in your personal life or your professional life.
- You must have the courage to let go of devious people from your life for your own good.
- You always deserve someone's trust, respect and love. If they can't offer that, look elsewhere.
- Understand that giving freely without expecting anything in return doesn't mean that you must hurt yourself.
- Trust people, yet put them through random checkpoints to see if they are trustworthy or not.
- A word of caution: do not form an opinion about anyone based on an isolated incident.
- Sometimes, you may not get a chance to solve an issue; it may remain a mystery. But that's alright. Let it be; everything in life is not in your control.

If you are facing any situation like the ones mentioned in these stories and are unable to trust someone, you may to do the following:

PAUSE AND REFLECT

- Keep an honest intention while evaluating people.
- Have an open mind while assessing a person's trustworthiness.
- Initially, give the person in question low-risk tasks.
- Check their responsiveness, credibility and the ability to live up to their tasks. Also, do a background-check about the person in question and try to speak to some references. If they pass these two tests, they are trustworthy.
- If they don't, let them go and find someone better to work with.

Let me know how your leadership qualities have changed after adopting the approach explained in this chapter. I'm keen to hear from you. You can write to me at connect@srijatabhatnagar.com

Life lesson: *Trust people, but never blindly. Remember, it is your job to trust fully, but it is their job to earn and keep that trust.*

✦✦✦

In the next chapter, we will discuss grief. Grief takes up a considerable amount of space in our hearts, significantly increasing the weight of our emotional baggage.

Did you lose a loved one to death? Do you still carry that person in your heart? How do you remember him or her – through happy memories, troubled memories, a pang of guilt or as regret for not doing something you intended to do when they were alive?

Let's ask our leaders and see what they have to say about it, shall we?

CHAPTER 8

Death and Beyond

Dr Kuiljeit Uppaal's experiences of dealing with her early-life crisis of polio, how she stood tall though society looked at her differently and how she dealt with her start-up setback tell us what kind of a leader she is. But what happens when such a leader loses her most prominent pillar of strength? How did she deal with the grief of losing one of the most precious persons in her life? Let's hear Kuiljeit's emotional narrative from her:

> *"Losing my dad to cancer was one of the most significant setbacks in my life. He was my role model and mentor in life, and he still is, because I have always believed that he is around even today. I always looked up to him. I look exactly like him – that's what everyone tells me – and among his three kids, I was the special one for him. I know that our bond was powerful. Also, due to the initial challenges I faced, he was the one who reached out to me and understood me quite well. Seeing him deal with life in a certain way over the years, I was silently imbibing a lot of his qualities. Even today, when I take some decisions, I often go back and think – 'If dad were here, how would he have done it?' and then decide accordingly.*
>
> *When we came to know he had cancer, it was a big jolt in my life. I was the first to receive the news that the cancer was already in the last stage and that we were going to lose him in a few months. I didn't let him go back to our home town, but made sure that he and my mother stayed with my husband, daughter and myself. My dad and mom remained with us till*

his last day. I was right there, standing by him when he took his last few breaths. I had promised him I wouldn't shed a tear all through his fight against the disease. I knew that cancer takes away everything from the person who is fighting it. My mother is a very emotional person; she had had so many breakdowns, that she needed someone who would be firmly standing by her side. I knew my dad was most concerned about my mom and about how she would respond to the fact that he wouldn't be around, soon. So I didn't want to weaken my father or increase his agony by shedding tears. And I chose to be strong! So much so, that my father nicknamed me 'his rock of Gibraltar'. No matter what happened, I didn't show him my moist eyes as long as he was alive. I was happy I could keep my promise, giving him strength until his last breath.

I miss him a lot. As a daughter and because I shared a deep bond and connection with him, there are moments when I miss him. I also have my vulnerable moments. I am okay with that, because God has made us emotional beings and we are supposed to use our emotions freely. Once in a while, I do have moist eyes when I think of dad. However, thanks to his tutoring since childhood, I learnt to deal with challenges and knew how to come out of them quickly. He taught me how to get out of a problem zone and step into a solution zone immediately. And so, I was back at work on the fourth day of his demise. Deep within, I was the worst-hit. But I knew that the only way to get out of it was to do what my dad would have typically done – because he always believed that while you are in this world, you are here for a purpose and you should never lose sight of that.

And so, as a way of showing him my respect and paying tribute to him, I honoured what he taught me – by getting back to work and keeping myself busy. Of course, in my silent moments, I would think of him and try to keep a smile on my face, because I always want to remember him that way. Music was the universal cord between us. Both of us were very fond of singing, and we had many jamming sessions together, where he would be on the harmonium and I would be on the tabla, singing along. We would go to concerts together; we bonded over music. That's why, ever since he left this world, I have been celebrating his birthday as a 'musical day'. In the morning, I pray for his departed soul and remember him and his teachings. And for the rest of the day, my music and I spend time together with Dad.

> **"I think people have different ways of dealing with grief. My idea of dealing with it is to give it a positive trajectory, wherein I remember him without crying or feeling bad about it."**

I tell my mom the same thing – that if you cry or feel bad about him, he is going to feel bad, too. When you lose a dear one, just remember that the person was dear to you and you had some fantastic times together. And so, the best way to keep the person in your heart is to reminisce those beautiful moments with a smile. It's great to keep remembering those incredible moments over and over again and let them become so prominent in your memory that the pain of losing the person fades away."

What a beautiful way to deal with grief! Only a balanced leader like Kuiljeit can think so beautifully about her irreversible loss. Kudos to her strength and the maturity to be able to deal with such an emotionally sensitive thing so positively and productively, remembering and cherishing her moments with her father.

> **PAUSE AND REFLECT**
>
> Have you lost someone precious? How do you choose to remember them?
>
> When you remember them, what do you think about, predominantly? Do you think of the good times spent with them or do you regret that you couldn't spend more time with them?
>
> Do you remember them with a smile on your face, or do you feel guilty that couldn't be there with them in their last moments?
>
> Also, did Kuiljeit's story help you in some way?
>
> Feel free to write to me at connect@srijatabhatnagar.com

I lost my father-in-law suddenly in 2017. Technically speaking, he was my father-in-law in relation. But Daddy (as I used to call him) was so much more than that to me. He was my best buddy, philosopher and guide. He was my most ardent cheerleader. We shared a bond so beautiful that it was beyond words. I could discuss any of my business ideas, professional escapades and even personal challenges with him without the fear of being judged or ridiculed. When I set out to be an entrepreneur, he would eagerly accompany me to the learning sessions for personal transformation. When he wrote a book, he made me his sounding board. In fact, I was the first one to read his half-baked manuscript!

He was an Army doctor and lived by the principle of genuinely helping others through his skills in Medicine. He was a paediatrician; yet, he chose to dedicate his life to the service of terminally ill cancer and AIDS patients. When I first met him, I was immediately impressed by his calm positivity, though he saw death every single day at his hospice. Over time, we bonded over various things, one of the most prominent among them being the passion for changing the world.

It was the day of Diwali, the festival of light and joy that is celebrated across India, in 2017. I had gone to the market to get flowers and other things to decorate our home with. When I returned home, my mother seemed rattled. Seeing her so disturbed, I started wondering what the matter was! Then she broke the news to me – Daddy had passed over a few mins ago.

I couldn't believe my ears! For a few minutes, I was dumbfounded. It took me some time to understand the news and process it. Daddy had gone to his brother's place to celebrate Diwali with them after a gap of many years. Everyone there was happy to have him; he was excited, too. In the morning, he read the newspaper, had a cup of tea, planned how he would decorate the house with lights and then, went to take a shower. He wanted to start decorating the house after his shower. But alas! That was not to be. A deadly stroke snatched him away from all of us.

Even though I was in an utter shock, my solution mindset kicked in. The first thing that came to my mind was that I would have to publish the book he was writing. It was my responsibility, and it would be a tribute to him. I asked my mother where my husband was. Because, even before *I* could grieve, I knew my husband needed my support at that time. And so, I chose to park my grief aside to support him through this unbearable loss of a parent.

The next few days passed in a daze. We all did what had to be done at that moment. I don't think any of us got a chance to grieve properly over Daddy's sudden demise.

I decided I wouldn't mourn his loss by crying, regretting or feeling guilty. Instead, I would do what he always wanted me to do – share my knowledge and skills with the world to transform human beings.

Daddy was very fond of writing. He wanted me to share my thoughts through my writing and to write a book eventually. And so, I took up formal writing. Today, two years after Daddy's demise, I am an avid blogger. I have written more than three hundred quotes, contributed to three published anthologies (one of which became a bestseller in its category) and written this book. Every time I write something, I think of how Daddy would have written it and then write accordingly.

Daddy's passing was a huge setback not only for me, but also for everyone else in our family. I chose to turn that setback into something where his memories would remain enshrined forever and would also help others transform their lives. Keeping his passion for transformation alive feels immensely satisfying.

It's crucial to let grief take shape in your mind and heart. In coaching people, we say that grief has stages. It starts with shock, then moves on to denial, then negotiation and finally, acceptance. Let yourself go through these stages one by one; take your time. Only one word of caution – DO NOT dwell in the early stages for a long time without moving to the next. Once you reach the acceptance stage, you will feel at peace – as if the person is in your heart and you can access them whenever you want, in your memories.

Learnings

+ Allow grief to take shape in your mind and heart.
+ Taking yourself through the different phases of grief allows your growth and liberation.
+ Do not dwell too long in the 'shock' and 'denial' phases of adjusting to grief. Move on to the 'negotiation' and 'acceptance' phases as soon as possible.
+ Just because you deal with grief in a particular manner, it doesn't mean others are dealing with it the wrong way. Everyone has different ways of coping with grief.
+ Make the memories of the most beautiful moments you spent with your lost ones so strong, that the pain of losing them almost fades away.
+ Keep their positive ideologies alive in your heart so firmly, that you keep the person alive in your life and work.

If you are a person going through grief right now or have lost someone significant in life and are unable to deal with your pain well, here is something you can do.

> **PAUSE AND REFLECT**
>
> Ask yourself the following:
>
> - How long has it been since they passed over?
> - Are you still adversely affected by their loss or have you reached the stage of acceptance?
> - How do you remember them in your thoughts?
> - What emotions do you go through when you remember them?
> - If they were alive, would they be happy to see you remember them the way you do?
> - Have you taken any action after their passing that you think would make them feel proud of you? If yes, would that make you a better version of yourself?
>
> You will see your entire point of view about loss and grief shift, and you will start appreciating the presence of your lost ones in your life.

Life lesson: *"When someone dies, only their physical presence is lost. But they remain in our thoughts, memories and actions forever."*

I got an opportunity to spend only a few years of my life in close contact with Daddy, but I was fortunate enough to imbibe some of his values that have made me a better human being. Today, I live a regret-free and guilt-free life.

✦ ✦ ✦

Have you ever faced a situation when you thought, "This is it. My life is over?"

In the next chapter, we will talk about some of the most devastating setbacks of our leaders' lives. What makes them all the more devastating is the severity of their impact on their lives, making them grapple with several things simultaneously. Some of these setbacks are so terrible that they will draw you to the edge of your seat, as you attempt to find out how on earth the affected people managed to come out of them! Some of them are so painful that *you* will feel the pain as well.

CHAPTER 9

Do or Die!

Most people go through a time in their lives when everything they have could be at stake: their job, reputation, finances, family, emotional balance, health, etc. could be threatened at the same time, making it a do-or-die situation for them. I have had my share of such setbacks, where I have thought that everything is lost. And so have other leaders.

Many people succumb to such setbacks, but leaders plough through the situation and come out triumphant. Extremely tough as it may be, they manage to bounce back from the terrible times, learning something in the process. On the contrary, others dwell in the situation and even perish sometimes, not knowing how to shrug off the damaging impact of the setback.

We already know that **Nikhil Chaudhary** faced multiple challenges in his life. Coincidentally, all of them happened almost at the same time, with each setback being intertwined with the others. He had to fight business failure, a financial challenge and one of his most devastating personal setbacks at the same time! This is what he says:

> *"One of my most significant setbacks came to me suddenly. My business was doing awesomely well, and my father had moved to India to support its growth. Unfortunately, after a few months of his move, the industry took a sudden turn southward. The mobile phone company I was a dealer of incurred huge losses. Hence, it closed down suddenly and the ripple effect of this hit my business hard. From being the best performing dealer to having no dealership was a rude shock, especially for my father.*

He always wanted to see me do well in life, as any loving parent would. This sudden fall of my business brought him face-to-face with an old fear of his.

Ages ago, a priest had told him that if he ever stayed with me, my career would be destroyed. When my dealership closed down, my father thought that the priest's words had come true. In that guilt-ridden stress, he started smoking excessively. This also led him to clinical depression and mental exhaustion. In no time, his health deteriorated so much that he began to have physical and psychological issues. Doctors advised severe treatments, including mild electric shocks.

Seeing him suffer like this, my grandmother suggested we shift my parents to Vrindavan, where she lived at that time. Even today, we have a house and a business there. Vrindavan is a small town in North India and is considered a sacred place in the Hindu religion. People go there to find peace of mind and solace. This vibrant town is famous for temples dedicated to Lord Krishna. My grandmother believed that a change of place would improve my father's mental and physical health and reduce his stress.

I agreed that this would be a good move. I was running around for work and had to manage my drying finances and many other challenging issues at the same time. Though I was looking after my dad, I could not give him 24/7 personal assistance and care. Also, I was living in Chennai at that time, and Tamil, the local language, was a barrier for my father. Therefore, he would socialise less with the locals.

On the contrary, we had family, friends and a large social circle in Vrindavan, and my dad knew Hindi very well. Several people visited my grandmother daily. Considering all this, I agreed to my grandmother's suggestion.

One day, after moving to Vrindavan, my dad went to visit a temple and never returned home. We searched fanatically in every possible place, and checked each nook and corner of the town. We enquired at police stations and hospitals, and even checked if he had drowned in the river. We asked everyone we would meet if they had seen him. But it was all in vain.

Eight years have gone by since that day, but there has been no sign of him anywhere. My mom still awaits his return. We have not stopped searching for him. Even today, all the sanyasis (holy men), jyothishis (astrologers), etc. say that he will return and I am happy about that. At least, this hope gives my mom strength. We still have dad's clothes, shoes and everything else intact. He may need them when he returns.

That was the worst time of my life. I blamed myself for calling him to India to be part of my business and then allowing him to go to Vrindavan. I thought if I hadn't called him to India, this wouldn't have happened.

I felt so terrible about this incident that I wanted to take my life. I remember looking up at the ceiling fan every night and thinking about it for hours. I wondered what if I had done this or that; dad would've been still around. I cursed the priest for planting that thought in dad's mind and held him accountable for our downfall, our troubles.

With my dad gone and mom living away, I had no reason left to work, make money, earn fame or do anything at all. I became almost philosophical. Nothing mattered anymore. The only questions that kept bothering me were, for whom should I live and what's the purpose of earning money? I was pretending to be unaffected by this incident; people around me never knew what exactly I was going through. On the outside, I was always smiling and full of energy. But inside, I was shattered. I cut down my social life drastically and stayed away from people because I could not afford to socialise. Nor I was interested in maintaining a social life. I completely shut myself off from the world.

Having the best parents in the world and having enjoyed an awesome childhood made it extremely difficult for me to go *through this terrible time. My dad had been a powerful influence on me since childhood; therefore, it became even more difficult for me to accept and acknowledge his disappearance.*

"Fortunately, I had two reasons to hang in there and spring back to life: one, my mom, who was already going through a terrible time. I couldn't have increased her agony. Two, my then-girlfriend and now-wife, who adored me, looked up to me and felt proud of me. Thanks to their presence and a huge amount of counselling and encouragement from my wife, I returned to regular life after a period of terrible suffering in the zone of self-criticism and self-pity."

Gosh, this is terrible! It affects us when we see our role model and anchor in life suffer like this. It does stop us momentarily from appreciating the life that we have got. But at the end of the day, it helps to concentrate on what we *have*, instead of what we have lost. It was because he did precisely this that Nikhil is a successful person today, professionally and personally.

Earlier in Chapter Two, we read about **Roger Cheetham**'s professional setback. That was nothing compared with what he had to go through a few years later. His beautiful and sorted life came to a standstill when an unexpected incident shattered his entire existence. Roger recalls that dark time with a shudder:

"On the 9th of June 2013, I took our black and white terrier, Jasper, out for a late evening walk, as usual. On our way back to the pub we were running and living in, three masked people suddenly ambushed me, wielding fenceposts and baseball bats. They were wearing hoodies, balaclavas and gloves. It was an extremely violent attack, where they came close to beating me to death. They kept thrashing me until they thought I was dead. They even turned their murderous attention to our beloved dog.

Fortunately, the first sickening blow broke Jasper's collar, and he was able to escape to safety.

Imagine going out for your usual evening walk and ending up being a target of attempted murder! Imagine all the physical injuries, lifelong disabilities and mental agony I had to bear because of this incident. Imagine my 13-year long career as a licensee/publican/bar manager being brought to an abrupt end. Imagine my wife and my 15-year-old daughter, seeing their loved one lying in the hospital bed, fighting to stay alive! It was an extremely traumatic experience – to nearly lose my life, to spend months after that in hospital and have a further lengthy period convalescing – all the while battling mental health implications also.

*Even stranger is the fact that even today, we don't know who those people were or why they targeted me. All we know is that I **was** their target and that they almost succeeded in killing me. For a long time, the thought kept bothering me, 'Why me?' I would write down the possible permutations and combinations to figure out who those three people could have been and on whose instructions they attacked me. Why would someone want to kill me?*

Even after thinking about it for two weeks, I still had a long list of fifty suspects and fifteen motives! That's when I woke up from my obsession with finding the WHY. I had to find the strength and resilience to tell myself that the police may find the culprits or they may not. But I couldn't carry on like this for the sake of my mental health.

"I told myself, what's the point in dwelling on the same thoughts? It's time I concentrated on my future, instead of always wondering why this had happened to me and destroying my psychological health."

I was encountering flashbacks and nightmares when I was asleep and even when I was awake. While I was never formally diagnosed *with PTSD (post-traumatic stress syndrome), I manifested nearly every symptom of it. A quote I often share when I give a talk is, 'The past is a place of reference and not a place of residence'. By this, I mean that when I had encountered such severe trauma, I couldn't just pretend that it had never happened and get back to where I was before. Instead, I needed to find some way to turn the negative into something positive. I started looking at it from the point of view that it happened **for** me, instead of it happened **to** me. And I realised that the story was no longer about me.*

I found it incredibly cathartic sharing this story, and I realised I needed to use it to help others. That's why I now frequently share my story from the stage.

My sole focus was to do everything it took to get the doctors, consultants and physiotherapists to allow me to return home. Being back home in familiar surroundings was all I dreamt about, all I aimed for and all I focused on for those three and a half months. But when I went back home, I found that the grass wasn't particularly greener on the other side, either. Yes, it felt good to be back. But because I had a large medical device, known as an external fixator, drilled through the bones at several places in my right lower leg, I wasn't able to walk upstairs or move around very much. My existence was limited to the living room, where I would feel incredibly lonely once again when my wife and daughter retired to bed. That loneliness and isolation were killing me. That's when I began wondering, 'What's the point in my surviving these months of painful treatments and agonising physiotherapy, if I was to live out the rest of my days confined to the living room?'

At this point, I realised I had to do something with my life, that, in the short term, would give me the much-needed self-fulfilment, and in the long term, would give me my life purpose. So many of us have a job or a business, but how many of us have a purpose in life? I also realised that, given this opportunity to start again after a 12 year-long career in IT and a 13-year long career as a licensee, I needed to do something more worthwhile with my life.

I therefore decided to share this experience to help other people; the victim in me transformed into a victor.

It wasn't easy for my family, either. For my wife, Clare and my daughter Tash, I was a difficult person to live with, because of the physical pain and emotional flashbacks. But once they realised that I had a strong purpose, they were both incredibly supportive. Those days, I would hesitate to go to any public place, for fear of being in the midst of people. I couldn't face them, because my confidence had been shattered. It's been quite a transformation, I'm sure you'll agree, from feeling like that back then, to now sharing this story in front of large audiences around the world to make a positive impact upon their lives.

During this time, Tash showed an immense level of maturity. She was studying for her General Certificate of Secondary Education (GCSE), a significant milestone for her. Like so many other 15-year-olds, she could have thought, 'What is the point in studying for my exams when I don't even know if my dad will live or not?' Instead, her view was that if I survived, she wanted me to see that she had done her best in the exams – to add her exam results to the ever-growing list of things I'm so proud of her for. Today, I couldn't be more pleased as I share with you, that despite everything she was dealing with, she left school with 11 GCSEs, all with high grades. It was an outstanding achievement, keeping in mind her tough situation and tender age."

What could be tougher than landing up as a victim of attempted murder and having to deal with the ensuing turmoil in life? That too, when you know your attackers must be roaming around freely, as they haven't been identified or caught!

But life can't stay still; it moves on. It's we who sometimes choose to stay put in our setback zone for longer than required. I love the way Roger decided to look past the toughest period of his life inspite of his physical and mental challenges. It is incredibly commendable, don't you think?

We read about **Brandi Benson**'s story of betrayal in Chapter Seven. If you remember, during the time Brandi had cancer, her husband wanted to leave her for another woman. Brandi was all of 24 years old and was just about starting her career in the US Army when she was diagnosed with cancer. She gives us details of what transpired:

> *"It was 2009. I was posted in war-torn Iraq as an American soldier. When I, as a 24-year-old soldier, was wondering how to battle the bullets, pallets and suicide bombings, a different kind of challenge arose in front of me, staring into my eyes.*
>
> *I spotted a lump on my left thigh one day. The lump started growing and in no time, I was diagnosed with Ewing Sarcoma cancer. This ailment challenged my profession, identity, faith, spirituality, marriage, relationships and the support system that I thought I had. It opened my eyes to life and showed me how fast life could be taken away from me.*
>
> *I was devastated and shaken to the core. I blamed my Karma for my ailment. I thought, 'Why me? Why does a 24-year-old girl need to go through such a painful experience? Was I a bad person? Did I do anything wrong to anyone? Did I deserve this?' As a young adult, I had my life charted out. I knew what I wanted to do, how my life would be, etc. Suddenly, this large black cloud called cancer cast a dark shadow on my life and declared, 'You know what? Whatever you had planned for yourself is not happening and will never happen.' I was taken aback. I used to play soccer in college and I was an athlete. I had dreams of appearing in the Olympics, as well. Now that a large portion of*

my thigh muscle would be taken away from my leg, I could never fulfil those dreams.

I was shattered beyond words.

It was a nightmarish experience. Apart from losing a big chunk of muscle, I was heavily losing hair, thanks to the heavy dosage of chemotherapy. Lying in my hospital bed, looking at my lump, I thought I was going to die. Everyone around me thought I was going to die, including some of the doctors. The priest would come every day and pray for my about-to-be-departed-soul, because he too thought I was going to die. My lawyer would come to meet me to know if I had made any changes in my Will, so that the formalities could be completed smoothly after I passed away. They came every single day. People kept reinforcing in me the thought that I was going to die.

It was my mom who became my rock of support. She helped me realise the true value of a robust support system. She never gave up; nor would she let me give up. Even when I was in my worst frame of mind and was rejecting the comforting words of cancer survivors, mom remained by my side. She became my reconstructive force when I was breaking inside. She quit her job and moved from Texas to Washington DC (where I was getting treated), not knowing if she would have money for food or a place to stay. She just decided that she was going to be in the hospital with me.

"Her strong support helped me wriggle out of self-pity. She would say, 'Brandi, you are a strong girl; this is not the end for you.' That's when I started telling myself that this could not be the end of me; this was just an experience, and it would pass."

I remember telling myself, 'I am going to get out of this nightmare soon. This experience is here to shake me up and to teach me how to become a better version of myself. The moment I shifted my thinking from 'cancer being a disease' to 'cancer being an experience', things started changing for me. Seeing the change, I started doing more of this; I was happier, laughing a lot, watching funny movies and finally, embracing cancer wholeheartedly with a promise to be fully cured one day. I knew this wasn't my entire story; this was going to be just a chapter in my life's book.

Once I accepted this, I felt that this setback had happened to me because I was strong enough physically, mentally and spiritually to handle it. I told myself that it was alright if whatever I had planned for myself was not happening; I'd just find something else to make my mark in life. I wasn't sure what it would be. But today, I understand that I was being prepared – through my experience – to enable the upliftment of others. Today, that episode doesn't feel like a setback anymore. It feels more like a setup for me to realise my true purpose and potential in life.

Before this episode, I was a shallow and self-centred person. This experience humbled me, it made me an empathetic person. It truly changed me as a person. The old Brandi died and a new Brandi was born. That's why I say, 'Cancer saved me!' People don't understand, but I genuinely feel that in every neuron of mine. The ailment helped me transform into a happier, fun-loving, helpful Brandi.

The cost of my treatment was around USD 1.5 million. I had to undergo chemotherapy over a hundred times. Fortunately, because I was in the military when I was diagnosed with cancer, I didn't have to pay a single penny for the treatment; the military bore all the expenses. I am immensely grateful to them for that. Otherwise, I would have been in debt now. The military took care of not only my treatment but also my mother's comfort, giving her a stipend and a place to stay. I shudder to think what I would have done if I hadn't been in the army when I contracted this ailment!"

Wow! That was a massive setback for Brandi – being afflicted by cancer at such a young age, having to alter all her plans and getting betrayed by her husband at the same time. This is what people mean when they say, "When it rains, it pours!"

I have noticed most of the time that it is not just one setback that appears. Along with it come other setbacks, too. But again, the more significant the setback, the more significant the opportunity to transform. What Brandi says is so true – the moment you change your mindset to see a setback as an opportunity for transformation, things start shifting immediately. Which is why, I believe that setback leadership is all about having the right mindset.

> **PAUSE AND REFLECT**
>
> What has been your do or die setback? How did you deal with it? Could you successfully leave it behind or are you still suffering from it?
>
> After listening to Nikhil, Roger and Brandi's stories, did you get some new ways to deal with your setback?
>
> Do write to me at connect@srijatabhatnagar.com to share your story. Who knows, I may feature you in my Setback Leadership blog, podcast or talk show!

My worst streak of setbacks hit me in 2013, immediately after I incorporated my first start-up. We incorporated EthnicShack in September of that year, and I fell ill in October. I landed up in hospital with severe stomach pain and vomiting, and was told that I had to be operated upon immediately, as I had a massive stone in my gallbladder. Generally, gallbladder stone surgeries are pretty simple, and the patient can be discharged the same day. But in my case, I had to suffer the pain for more than 40 hours, thanks to a total shutdown in the city. Also, because of continuous vomiting, I was dehydrated, which aggravated the situation further.

Fortunately, a world-renowned gastroenterologist was attending to me, and he ensured that I was taken care of well. Even so, where other patients could go home the same today, it took me five days to regain full consciousness and strength. For the next three months, I recuperated, keeping my newly formed start-up aside.

Anyway, after that initial speed-breaker, I started working on my company, met more than 500 artisans and craftsmen along the way, travelled all over India and understood various arts and crafts well. We started co-creating products that would be suitable for the urban Indian market. At the same time, I was also building the sales and marketing avenues for the venture. We tried selling our products through our website, other e-commerce platforms, offline exhibitions and pop-ups. Also, we took up a big office for storing our products and photographing them.

That's where we went wrong.

We spent our capital on something that wouldn't provide us with direct results. Instead of paying a significant amount of money for an expensive office, we should have invested it on market research and in understanding the customer better. What we didn't realise is that India wasn't yet ready for the 'handmade, handcrafted' revolution. We were early in the market, and as we were bootstrapped, we didn't have a deep pocket for creating awareness on a large scale.

We tried every possible way we could to ensure that sales and the number of customers grew. But our overheads were killing us. So eventually, we had to let go of our office. But by then, it was already too late. We had lost INR 2.5 million. This broke our back, and we were not able to sustain the venture anymore. And so, we decided to shut it down.

It wasn't easy for me to close down the company I had started with such love and enthusiasm. It felt as if I was killing my child. I was already very depressed. On top of that, people started blaming me for this failure. Being the founder and CEO of the company, I had to face everyone's wrath for the debacle. Our vendors kept calling me for payments; my peers started gossiping and saying I was a failure. Even my business partner put the entire blame on me. Many people began avoiding me. When my relatives asked my parents what I did for a living, my parents would lie to them. On the other hand, our artisans kept requesting me to continue with the business.

My entire family was disappointed with me. They had told me not to quit my job and get into business; they had told me not to take the risk. But I had chosen to take that risk anyway and to walk down an unknown path.

Eventually, I started blaming myself. My self-worth deteriorated drastically. I went into a zone where the whole day, I would blame myself for every small thing that went wrong in my life. Or, I'd blame everyone around me.

It was so bad that I wondered what the point in living this life was. I thought I must die. I thought I was useless. I couldn't be a competent professional, a good daughter, a good wife or a good mother. I was a burden – not only to the world at large, but also to my family.

With these thoughts in my mind, I went to the pharmacy one day and bought a bunch of sleeping pills. I thought these would be sufficient for me to take my life. Keeping those pills in my bag, I wandered around the city, thinking about various things for more than two weeks. My family had no clue about what was going on in my mind. They thought I was living a very comfortable life with all the comforts; then there was no way I could be unhappy, could there? My relationship with my husband deteriorated, as well; we would fight every now and then, saying bitter things to each other that we should have avoided.

I wasn't even aware that I was sinking into depression. After a few weeks of this turmoil in my head, I somehow realised that something was drastically wrong with me. That's when I read a report somewhere that there is no shame in visiting a psychiatrist when things didn't feel right in your head. I decided to take one last chance. If things didn't improve, I would end my life.

On my first visit to the psychiatrist, she placed a condition that she would see me only if I brought my husband along. That was the worst situation I have ever faced in my life! No one in my family was aware that I had visited a psychiatrist. And I knew my husband would be devastated if he came to know this. I couldn't put him through such a shock. He would start blaming himself immediately. Thinking of all this, I pleaded with my psychiatrist to relax her rule. But she refused to budge.

Reluctantly, I had to tell my husband about it. As expected, he was in shock and despair. He was unable to understand why I was going through this, and what my need to see a psychiatrist was.

I urged him to accompany me to her clinic just once – if he wanted to see me alive. That's how my recovery started. Within three months of regular counselling and therapy, I started gaining my self-confidence and self-worth. As I improved my relationship with myself, my relationship with my family, husband and daughter improved, too. But it still took me around 18 months to return to my usual self. I concentrated on developing my skills. Slowly, I became fiercely confident again and went on to start another business.

Imagine going through physical, professional, emotional, financial and relationship troubles all at the same time, along with depression. My troubles were so intense that I could have just perished!

What kept me afloat were these: my journaling habit, my sense of responsibility towards my daughter, the constant therapy and counselling, the support of my husband and multiple mentors and coaches who helped me see the situation pragmatically. And finally, my own desire to stay afloat and bounce back to life was a big source of strength.

> Now, when I read my journal from those days, I laugh at it. Those feelings, thoughts and situations have remained stuck in the book, while I have moved far ahead in life.

Learnings

Let's take stock of the most prominent learnings from the stories we read in this chapter:

- ✦ Self-pity and self-criticism are the deadliest of pits you can fall into when you are going through a setback. Know that your going through a devastating setback is not because you intentionally wanted to go through it. And so, there is no need to criticise yourself.
- ✦ Remember that you have various strong reasons to stay afloat even when you go through a tough situation – even if the setback is one that could sink you forever. You have to find those reasons to stay afloat.
- ✦ There is no point in asking, "Why me?" The quicker you get this question out of your mind, the faster your recovery from your problems will be.
- ✦ The more significant the setback, the better the chances of a 'brand new you' being born.
- ✦ And the most significant learning of all – no matter what setback has hit you, it's *you* who can *decide* to look beyond it for your growth. You can keep those setbacks in your memory as badges of honour.

If you are going through one of the toughest times of your life now, I encourage you to do the following:

> **PAUSE AND REFLECT**
>
> - Start journaling each of your thoughts – good, bad and ugly – freely.
> - Look for support in your family – people with whom you can share your fears, inhibitions and pains without the fear of being judged.
> - If the situation warrants it, look for experts who can help you out of this confusing situation.
> - I know it is tough, but gather the courage to go out and share your challenges with others.
> - Hire a coach or see a psychiatrist and take necessary action to come out of this quicksand as soon as you can.
>
> There is no shame in seeing a psychiatrist or hiring a coach. If professional sportspersons can have a coach to work on their performance, why can't you have a coach for *your* performance? In fact, top sportspersons even have mind coaches, who work on their attitude and mindset towards life.

Remember, our physical performance *and* mental performance need training. It is essential to train our mind just like we train our body. It's high time we stop feeling stigmatised for having to train or coach our mind. It is a good idea for you to hit the mind gym – hire people who can help your mind exercise and keep it sharper, stronger and more focussed.

Life Lesson: ***Robust software is needed to run strong hardware. Similarly, a fearless and resilient mind is needed to run a strong body.***

I always thought I was strong. But the several setbacks I have encountered made me realise that no matter how strong we think we are from the outside, if we have a weak mind, we will go nowhere.

Don't you agree?

✦✦✦

Final Words – Let's Recap and Practice the Techniques

While reading this book, you would have had your aha! moments. If so, it is time to put those moments into action.

I am a big believer in action. The moment someone comes to me with a setback, my mind starts thinking about a solution. That's because I have experienced setbacks every step of the way in my life, and I know that the moment we take action, we move forward. This is also true for all the leaders I have met and worked with in the past 20 years – and even in the lives of those featured in this book. Had they not taken any action, they wouldn't be as successful as they are today.

I invite you to identify three areas of your life where you want to change your reality and start taking action that moves you forward from where you are now. Each step counts. People always begin slowly, taking one step at a time. And eventually, those steps will make a stable path forward for them.

If you found some golden nuggets in this book, I encourage you to write those down and follow them sincerely for a minimum of 21 days (studies have found that for any behaviour to crystallise into a habit, you need to perform it for 21 consecutive days). Make sure it becomes your thinking pattern. Ultimately, habit creation is in our hands. Once the new habits form, the old unproductive habits will automatically melt away.

Let me share some of *my* favourite nuggets from the stories featured in this book.

- "Setbacks are like friends of ours; they come into our lives to teach us something. Embrace them." – Dr Kuiljiet Uppaal
- "My setbacks weren't setbacks; they were set up for me to do and experience what I am experiencing today." – Brandi Benson
- "An optimist finds a solution in every situation, while a pessimist finds a situation in every solution." – Roger Cheetham
- "It's the hard that makes it good. If it were easy, everyone would do it." – Lauren Powers
- "I had stopped loving myself, simply because someone else had stopped loving me. And because I had stopped loving myself, I felt the world had stopped loving me." – Katherine Wintsch
- "Nature has everything in abundance. It's we who need to know how to route it right and use it for a positive impact." – Sagar Amlani
- "My philosophy is that we can go through any shitty experience in life; it's *our* choice whether we want to be a victim or a victor." – Diaz Richards
- "The financial problems in my life were an outcome of my choices, and my financial freedom is also an outcome of my choices. Attitude matters! Money follows, inwards or outwards." – Nikhil Chaudhary

Once you have chosen your favourite nuggets, pick one at a time and start repeating it to yourself every day for the next 21 days. Once that nugget has been drilled into your belief system, select the next one and repeat this task.

A mindset that has helped me move into the solution zone or solution mode quickly is to ask myself, "*Can I do something about this problem now?*" If the answer is yes, I immediately take action. If the answer is no, I ask another question, "*Can I do something about it after a week?*" If the answer to this is yes, I go back to the problem after a week and sort it out. However, if the answer is no, I ask myself the third question, "*When can I do something about this problem?*"

Based on the answer, I set up a reminder on my calendar and go back to the problem on that particular date. And if I cannot solve the problem because it's beyond my reach or understanding, I simply stop thinking about it.

Looking at things objectively and always keeping a solution mindset has helped me immensely. How about you? What kind of mindset would you like to cultivate? That will determine if you are a setback victim or a setback leader.

✦✦✦

About the Author

Srijata Bhatnagar is a professional speaker, a life coach and an entrepreneur. She has inspired more than 10,000 people through her talks, one-to-one coaching sessions, videos and quotes. The fact that she was initially an employee and then turned entrepreneur helps her see both sides of the coin. With more than 20 years of experience (building two businesses, speaking professionally and coaching numerous companies and individuals), she is a repository of transformational knowledge.

Srijata has been through various kinds of setbacks in her life, thanks to her inquisitive nature, her circumstances, her mistakes and the path that life has taken her down. Given the nature of her work, she meets and works with leaders from many industries – leaders who have also been through setbacks.

Srijata shares her unique, empowering and powerful points of view with her audiences. She delivers her message and coaches people through engaging real-life stories, amusing incidents, self-deprecating humour, her personal experiences, and at times, even a narration of painful setbacks. Her forte lies in guiding businesses and individuals to rise above their fears, doubts and limiting beliefs, and achieve holistic success in their professions and lives. No wonder she is an expert in the area of Setback Leadership.

Srijata is known as the "Iron Lady who can cry, too". Be sure to ask her how she got this name. There is a fascinating story behind it!

You can read more about her on her website www.srijatabhatnagar.com and write to her at connect@srijatabhatnagar.com. She'd love to hear from you.

✦✦✦